insight text guide

Adam Kealley

Jasper Jones

Craig Silvey

First published in 2021, reprinted in 2022, 2023.

Insight Publications Pty Ltd
3/350 Charman Road
Cheltenham VIC 3192
Australia
Tel: +61 3 8571 4950
Fax: +61 3 8571 0257
Email: books@insightpublications.com.au

www.insightpublications.com.au

A catalogue record for this book is available from the National Library of Australia

Craig Silvey's Jasper Jones / Adam Kealley

Adam Kealley asserts the moral right to be identified as the author of this work.

ISBNs:
9781922525376 (print)
9781922525383 (digital)
9781922525390 (bundle: print + digital)

Cover design by Melisa Paredes

Printed by Markono Print Media Pte Ltd

contents

CHARACTER MAP

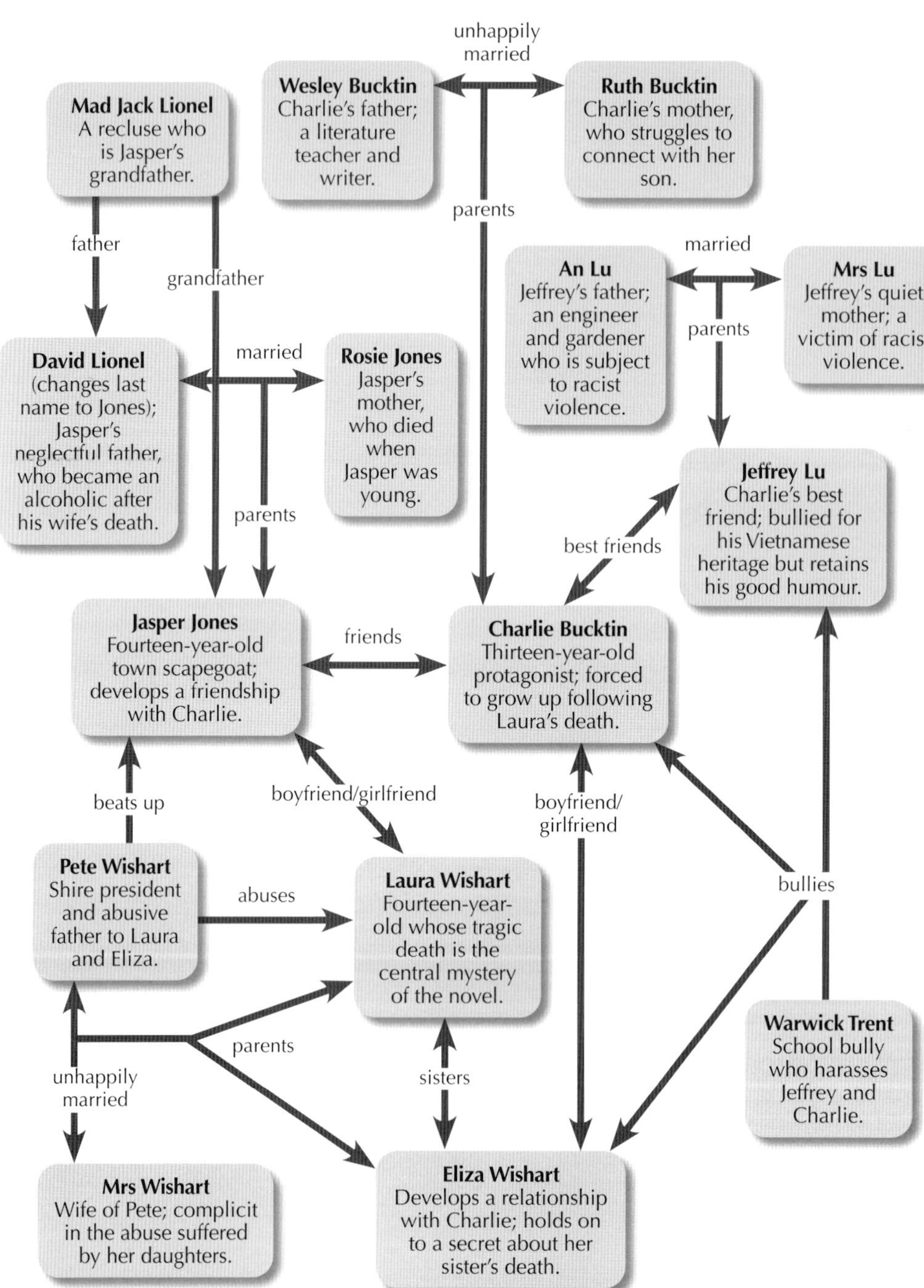

OVERVIEW

About the author

Originally from Dwellingup, a small town in Western Australia, Craig Silvey now lives in the port city of Fremantle. He was born in 1982 and wrote his first novel, *Rhubarb*, when he was nineteen (although it wasn't published until 2004), followed by a children's book, *The World According to Warren,* which was published in 2007. As a full-time author he is now occupied with research, writing, speaking engagements and festival appearances. In addition, Silvey is a singer and songwriter with the band 'The Nancy Sikes!'

Jasper Jones (2009) is Silvey's second novel and has been both a critical and commercial success. In 2017, it was adapted into a feature film directed by Rachel Perkins; Silvey shared screenwriting credits with Shaun Grant. The novel was also adapted for the stage in 2014 by Kate Mulvaney, and produced by various theatre companies.

In 2012, Silvey wrote a novella for younger readers titled *The Amber Amulet*. His third novel, *Honeybee* (2020) caused some controversy due to Silvey's choice to write from the perspective of a troubled transgender teenager, Sam.

Craig Silvey has been twice nominated as one of the Best Young Australian Novelists by *The Sydney Morning Herald*, winning the award in 2005 for *Rhubarb*. *Jasper Jones* has been Silvey's greatest critical success, short-listed for numerous awards and winning several, both nationally and internationally, between 2009 and 2012, including the Western Australian Premier's Book Awards (2009 Fiction joint winner), the Indie Book of the Year, the Australian Book Industry Awards (ABIA) and, in the US, the American Library Association Best Fiction for Young Adults award and the Michael L Printz Honor Award for young adult literature.

Synopsis

Jasper Jones is set in 1966 in Corrigan, a small rural mining town. Thirteen-year-old Charlie Bucktin is trying to sleep when town outcast Jasper Jones comes to his window begging for help. Afraid but flattered, Charlie follows Jasper to a clearing in the bush where he discovers the body of a young girl, Laura Wishart, hanging from a tree. Jasper persuades Charlie to help hide the body in a nearby dam. The clearing is Jasper's personal hideaway, where he escapes both the violence and neglect of his father and the racism of the other townsfolk. He explains to Charlie that he was friends with Laura, daughter of the shire president, and that, due to the town's racism and prejudice, he will be blamed for her death. Jasper believes the killer is Mad Jack Lionel, a mysterious recluse who supposedly killed another young woman years earlier.

Charlie is best friends with Jeffrey Lu, an intelligent, humorous and cricket-loving Vietnamese boy. Jeffrey is also a victim of the town's racism, heightened by the ongoing Vietnam War. Charlie develops a crush on Eliza Wishart, who is grieving the disappearance of her sister, and the two begin a relationship. Charlie begins researching famous murderers and cases of missing children, trying to solve Laura's apparent murder.

Through a series of events, Charlie learns the harsh realities of life. Jeffrey's parents suffer racially motivated attacks and Jasper reveals his history of neglect and abuse. When Jasper and Charlie finally confront Jack, they realise he is a lonely and misunderstood man – and Jasper's grandfather. The woman Jack killed was Jasper's mother, Rosie, who died in a car crash when she had appendicitis and Jack was driving her to the hospital. Charlie discovers that his mother is having an affair and that his parents' marriage is loveless and miserable. Eliza confesses to Charlie that she feels responsible for her sister's death, having followed Laura to the clearing and watched her hang herself. She shows Charlie and Jasper a letter in which Laura reveals that she has been sexually abused by her father. Overcome with grief, Jasper dives into the dam. He is rescued by Charlie, who realises Jasper's self-assurance is a mask.

Charlie's mother leaves town, leaving him in the care of his father, Wesley. Charlie feigns stealing peaches from Jack's tree, in a bargain to stop Warwick Trent bullying him, while Eliza confronts her parents with Laura's abuse. In a cathartic act of vengeance, she burns down the family home and Charlie realises that Jasper will once again be blamed for the crime. Jasper, however, simply disappears, and the novel concludes with Charlie and Eliza watching the conflagration.

Character summaries

Charlie Bucktin

Protagonist Charlie Bucktin is a precocious, intelligent but insecure thirteen-year-old. In a town where status is correlated with sporting prowess, the non-athletic Charlie is an outsider who enjoys studying, writing and reading, especially American literature by authors such as Mark Twain and Truman Capote.

Jasper Jones

Jasper Jones is one of Corrigan's many outcasts, ostracised for being half-Aboriginal and the son of a dysfunctional father. The scapegoat for many local crimes and misdemeanours, Jasper knows he will be the number-one suspect in Laura's death. He appears to be mature and self-assured, but is really as uncertain and lonely as Charlie.

Eliza Wishart

Composed, intelligent and beautiful, Eliza Wishart is Laura's younger sister, and Charlie's love interest. Eliza feels guilty for not saving her sister but reveals strength of character when she stands up to her parents and holds them to account for their actions. The implication that Eliza burns down her family home with her father inside reveals a dangerous edge at odds with her gentleness.

Jeffrey Lu

A year younger than Charlie, Jeffrey Lu is Charlie's best friend, the irrepressible and cricket-mad son of Vietnamese immigrants. Despite the prejudice he experiences, Jeffrey retains his quirky humour; he and Charlie trade witticisms and banter throughout the novel.

Mad Jack Lionel

Jack Lionel is a reclusive old man and another of Corrigan's outcasts. Town mythology paints him as a crazy murderer. Jasper feels threatened by Jack, who shouts out his name every time he sees the boy. When Jasper and Charlie confront Jack, they learn he is Jasper's grandfather. He initially rejected his son, David, for marrying Rosie, an Aboriginal woman, but eventually developed a close relationship with her after she gave birth to Jasper. Unfortunately, Jack was responsible for Rosie's death when his car crashed while he was driving her to the hospital when she had appendicitis. The accident tore the family apart and Jasper grew up unaware of his connection to Jack.

Wesley Bucktin

Wesley (also called Wes) is Charlie's father, a literature teacher and writer. Wes is wise, calm and just – qualities that Jasper also values in Charlie. Although he adores his father, Charlie is frustrated by his passive behaviour and resents the fact that Wes keeps some things secret from him, such as the novel he is writing and the dysfunction within his marriage.

Ruth Bucktin

Focalised through Charlie's eyes, his mother Ruth is depicted as unreasonable and petty, resenting her husband's emotional distance and blaming him for the dullness of their small-town life. When her extramarital affair is discovered by Charlie, she leaves her son and husband and returns to the city.

Laura Wishart

Eliza's older sister, Laura was in a relationship with Jasper Jones at the time of her death. Jasper values Laura's sensitivity and thoughtfulness, and the two had talked about leaving Corrigan together. After being sexually abused by her father and becoming pregnant, Laura takes her own life, although Jasper and Charlie initially assume she has been murdered.

Warwick Trent

A member of the cricket team, Warwick taunts both Charlie and Jeffrey, his bullying sometimes becoming physical. He is forced to re-evaluate his treatment of them after Jeffrey's success on the cricket pitch and Charlie's apparent act of courage in stealing peaches from Mad Jack's tree.

David Jones

David changed his surname from Lionel to Jones when his father, Jack, would not accept his marriage to Rosie. David is Jasper's alcoholic and abusive father. His neglect means that Jasper is largely forced to care for himself, stealing necessities to live.

Minor characters

Rosie Jones: Jasper's mother, an Aboriginal woman whose death precipitated David's slide into depression and alcoholism.

An Lu: Jeffrey's father, a devoted gardener whose front yard is destroyed in a racist act of vandalism.

Mrs Lu: Jeffrey's mother, a kind and loving woman who is attacked by Sue Findlay.

Sue Findlay: distressed by her son being conscripted to serve in the Vietnam War, she attacks Mrs Lu in an anti-Vietnamese rage.

Pete Wishart: the racist, cruel and bullying shire president, and father of Laura and Eliza, who abuses his eldest daughter.

Mrs Wishart: wife of Pete Wishart and mother of Laura and Eliza, who initially ignores or refuses to believe that her husband is abusing Laura.

BACKGROUND & CONTEXT

Historical and social setting

Jasper Jones is set in 1966 in Corrigan, a fictional small mining town in the southwest of Western Australia whose society is patriarchal, largely monocultural and working class. As Charlie describes it, 'The mine employs most people, and the power station herds in the rest, which means there isn't much of a class divide' (p.8). The 'social currency' is sport, and thus Charlie's bookishness and intelligence only brings him 'ire' and 'resentment' from his peers (p.8). The bullying he and Jeffrey are subjected to is often homophobic. Despite his admiration for his father Wes, a literature teacher and writer, it is clear that Charlie has absorbed the town's masculine mores, frequently using the pejorative term 'pansy' in reference to his sandals and characterising his own behaviour as 'girlishness' (p.3).

Corrigan is a place dominated by racism and misogyny, where powerful men protect one another and turn a blind eye to corruption. It is this culture that allows the police to beat Jasper, the shire president to abuse his daughter, and townsfolk to vilify the Lu family, all with little fear of reprisal. Anyone who is different is ostracised: Charlie and Eliza for their academic prowess, Jasper and Jeffrey for their races.

The 1960s is often portrayed as the decade in which Western Australia lost its innocence. Events such as the Vietnam War, the civil rights movement and the crimes of Eric Edgar Cooke, Perth's notorious serial killer, resulted in a shift in social climate. No longer could the public remain happily ignorant, when the extent of others' suffering was being so sharply brought into focus.

The Vietnam War

The Vietnam War lasted from 1955 until 1975, eventually encompassing Vietnam, Laos and Cambodia. Officially, it was a conflict between North Vietnam, supported by communist powers including the Soviet Union and China, and South Vietnam, supported by the United States, Australia, Thailand and other anti-communist allies. Australia's ten-year involvement in the war (1962–72) was contentious. Initially, Australians were supportive of the war effort, believing it necessary to prevent the spread of communism. However, after the introduction of conscription (mandatory enlistment of young men into the military) and as stories of atrocities against Vietnamese civilians emerged, public opinion began to change, with many calling for an end to Australia's involvement. In Chapter 5, Charlie notes that 'three young men from Corrigan have been called up for National Service' (pp.164–5).

In the 1960s, the time in which *Jasper Jones* is set, fewer than 2000 Vietnamese people lived in Australia, making the Lu family something of an oddity, particularly for a rural town. An Lu is an engineer at the mine and, although his beautiful garden is admired by many, the Vietnam War raises tensions and foments suspicion about the family. Jeffrey is pejoratively referred to as 'Cong' (p.80) – a reference to the Viet Cong, communist guerrillas who fought with North Vietnam against US and Australian troops – and is excluded from the cricket team, while Mrs Lu is scalded with hot tea and abused with 'the most horrible words' (p.168) by Sue Findlay, whose son has been conscripted. In another act of racially motivated violence, An Lu's garden is vandalised and he is beaten by four local men, including Mick Thompson and James Trent, who label An a 'red rat' (p.267), a reference to being a communist spy.

The 1967 Referendum

The 1967 Referendum asked the Australian voting public whether Aboriginal and Torres Strait Islander people should be counted in the census and whether the Commonwealth could make laws regarding them. Over ninety per cent of eligible Australians voted 'Yes'. The Referendum allowed the federal government to change the Australian Constitution and introduce laws to address racial inequality. It was the first step in recognising the structural discrimination experienced by First Nations peoples since settlement.

Prior to the Referendum, the Constitution did not give First Nations peoples the same rights as other Australians. Laws in various states and territories limited their right to vote, own property, marry, move freely, drink alcohol and even care for their own children. They were often unfairly targeted by authorities. When Jasper is detained and beaten up by the police, Charlie asks, 'Are they allowed to do that?' (p.177), to which Jasper replies, 'They don't need a reason, mate. Besides, who am I going to report it to, anyway?' (p.178).

The 2008 Apology to Australia's Indigenous Peoples

On 13 February 2008, then Prime Minister Kevin Rudd offered a formal apology to Aboriginal and Torres Strait Islander peoples for their 'grief, suffering and loss' at the hands of the government, particularly those affected by Australia's longstanding policy of removing children from their families – the Stolen Generations (Rudd 2008a, b). Since then, National Sorry Day (26 May) has been observed to acknowledge the Stolen Generations and the strength and resilience of First Nations peoples, and to promote ongoing reconciliation. The national importance of the apology is alluded to in the novel when Charlie reflects on the significance of the word 'sorry' carved into a tree, and notes that it is 'the wake of a misdeed … the crippling ripple of consequence' (p.263) and that an apology 'bridges the gap' (p.263) between offerer and recipient. This is language significant to the movement for equality in terms of the 2000 Walk for Reconciliation across Sydney Harbour Bridge and the ongoing implementation of the National Agreement on Closing the Gap (an agreement aimed at addressing the disadvantages experienced by First Nations Australians).

The Southern Gothic tradition

The American Southern Gothic is a literary tradition that has long fascinated Silvey, who believes it to be a genre that 'lend[s] itself well to the Australian condition' (Silvey n.d.). The Southern Gothic uses motifs of the macabre, madness, decay and horror to examine present-day values and myths of the southern states of the US in light of the region's history of slavery, racism and patriarchy.

Writers of this genre mentioned in the novel include Eudora Welty, William Faulkner, Flannery O'Connor and Harper Lee. Lee's famous novel *To Kill a Mockingbird*, with its naive narrator Scout Finch and its themes of small-town corruption, scapegoating and racial inequality, is a clear source of inspiration for Silvey. Scout comes to understand the dark undercurrents of her town as her father Atticus, a lawyer, defends an African American man falsely accused of raping a white girl. Many of Silvey's characters have parallels with Lee's cast: Charlie and his father Wesley standing for Scout and Atticus Finch, Mad Jack Lionel for the reclusive Boo Radley and Jasper Jones for the falsely accused Tom Robinson.

GENRE, STRUCTURE & LANGUAGE

Genre

Jasper Jones does not fit neatly into one genre. It has won prizes for both literary fiction and young adult literature; its key themes are those of a bildungsroman (a coming-of-age novel), while the titular hero embodies ideas associated with the Australian Gothic.

The Australian Gothic

The Australian Gothic has its origins in Australian colonial literature. New migrants writing in an alien environment expressed their anxiety and sense of displacement by transferring Gothic literature's ghoulishness to Australian settings such as isolated homesteads and dangerous wilderness.

The Australian Gothic employs many conventions of the traditional Gothic, such as marginalised or outcast characters; symbols of decay and corruption that reflect moral degeneracy; imagery of liminality (spaces and transitions) or unclear borders; themes of secrets, the taboo, crime and violence; literal or psychological hauntings; and a focus on the underbelly of small communities. The grotesque events of Australian Gothic novels are intended to draw attention to the unpleasant or hidden realities of the society they critique.

The genre continues to reflect the ongoing uncertainties of white Australians' place within the continent, as well as fears that urban settings 'could be just as chilling as the outback' (Turcotte 1998), due to their veneer of respectability. The position of First Nations voices within the Australian Gothic is complex. In early examples, their presence was often rendered as either evil or haunting, unsettling the white protagonists. In more recent times, writers such as Alexis Wright and Kim Scott have employed the Australian Gothic genre to voice their own experiences of horror arising from colonisation.

Although ostensibly focused on Charlie, as he comes to terms with the grim realities of the adult world, intra-familial abuse and violence, *Jasper Jones* also engages with the racism and prejudice experienced by its First Nations characters. Jasper occupies a marginal position in relation to Corrigan, effectively haunting its population through his ill-deserved reputation. Silvey's decision to set the novel before the 1967 Referendum is significant, as prior to this event First Nations people were officially denied personhood, relegating them, in effect, to the position of ghosts.

The bildungsroman

The bildungsroman (plural: bildungsromane), often referred to as a coming-of-age story, is a novel that charts the psychological or moral growth of a protagonist from youth to adulthood.

Typical tropes within the contemporary bildungsroman include a naive protagonist who has feelings of alienation and uncertainty; conflict with authorities such as parents; a gradual increase in independence and empathy for others; tests of character in which the protagonist must re-evaluate their own moral code; characters who teach or guide the protagonist; physical and emotional journeys; rites of passage into adulthood, such as sexual experiences; and themes of self-discovery and personal identity.

The naive protagonist is usually cast out of childhood innocence by an event that rattles their solipsistic (self-centred) world view and puts them at odds with society and the established order. They undertake a journey, facing various trials that test their character or morality. Through rites of passage, they gain an adult understanding of the world and their place within it, equipping them to participate in adult life and return to society. This journey can be either positive, as they come to better understand themselves and how to navigate the adult world, or negative, as they realise the flawed nature of the adult world and must compromise in order to fit in. Thus, their new 'maturity' is simply learning how to be accepted by those in positions of authority or power: adults. Today, bildungsromane may instead feature protagonists who resist this and challenge or escape from corrupt authorities, or establish alternative societies.

Jasper Jones clearly exhibits the conventions of this genre. Charlie's innocence is shattered by the discovery of Laura's body and his growing awareness of corruption. In juggling conflicting loyalties, Charlie must evaluate his own moral character. He learns that life is a series of moral compromises, and that true courage is learning to live with the weight of this knowledge. It is this awareness that allows him to overcome his initial desire to run away from Corrigan, and instead find a way to live with its corruption.

Structure

Jasper Jones follows a linear, chronological structure, although the letter written by Laura Wishart (read to Charlie by Eliza) provides the backstory to her suicide, and Jack Lionel relates the history of Jasper's parents and Rosie's death.

The novel is divided into nine chapters. The first introduces the major characters and the inciting incident – Charlie's encounter with Laura Wishart's body. The central conflict is established, largely focused on the question of who killed Laura, but also Charlie's own inner conflict as he wrestles with his sense of morality and as his belief in established authorities, such as the police, is tested. In each chapter, Charlie is confronted with incidents that shake his world view, as he realises people's capacity for corruption and cruelty – both petty and profound. These grim lessons are counterbalanced by his developing romance with Eliza, and his deepening friendships with Jeffrey and Jasper.

The climax of the novel occurs in Chapter 7, where the circumstances of Laura's death are finally revealed. The final two chapters are brief, wrapping up the details of how the various characters settle back into life. The (mostly) long chapters and the relatively short time span of the novel – one summer – reflect the intensity of this life-changing period for Charlie.

Narrative point of view

Jasper Jones is narrated in the first person, from the perspective of Charlie Bucktin, a precocious but somewhat naive thirteen-year-old. Like the authors he admires, he is frequently an observer of the world around him. This enables him to narrate the actions of others in convincing detail as well as to observe sometimes horrifying scenes, such as the encounter with Laura's dead body.

The first-person point of view gives the reader intimate access to Charlie's anxieties and moral conflicts, whether they be his fear of insects or the dilemma of hiding Laura's body to protect Jasper. A significant portion of the narration is given over to Charlie's internal thoughts as he interrogates all he observes.

Language

Colloquialism and eye-dialect

Capturing a distinctly Australian voice, Silvey makes significant use of colloquialisms, such as 'bloody disgrace' (p.80), and eye-dialect (spelling words as they are phonetically pronounced), such as 'carn' for 'come on' (p.198) and 'Gissa hand' for 'give us a hand' (p.52). Sometimes this is distorted by the boys for comic effect, such as Jeffrey's 'Cheeses Christ arrrrrr Larrrrrd' (p.102) or his exaggeration of his stereotyped accent in 'me so *solly*' (p.78). This adds a sense of verisimilitude (realism) to the novel, and also reveals that language is often used by characters to mask their true fears and anxieties: Jeffrey deflecting racial abuse, Charlie adopting stereotypical masculine behaviours in contrast to his sensitive and highly literate self, and Eliza adopting her Golightly accent when she is 'particularly low or sad' (p.376).

Non-standard syntax

In Chapter 7, Charlie's recount of Eliza's confession about Laura and her death is one continuing paragraph almost twelve pages long, which frequently uses short or fragmentary sentences and repeated variations of the compressed phrase 'thisiswhathappened' (p.329). This gives this section of the novel a heightened pace, as if the sentences, with their horrifying revelations, are tumbling out of Charlie's mind, 'fizzing and spraying' (p.329). It clearly reflects Charlie's agitated state as he tries to grapple with a series of confronting realisations. A similar use of fragmented syntax is evident in Chapter 1 (p.12), when Charlie sees Laura's dead body for the first time, another moment in which he struggles to comprehend the world.

Figurative language and symbols

Silvey frequently employs figurative language devices, such as metaphors, similes and allusions to American writers such as Harper Lee and Mark Twain. Some of these become motifs; for example, a **bubble** initially represents the fragile world of childhood innocence, before being used to describe the clearing itself, which somewhat ironically becomes a haven for Charlie and Eliza. Also the inflamed appendix that kills Rosie is 'a bubble ready to burst' (p.315). The snowdome motif represents Charlie's world being shaken up after Laura's death.

Charlie's fear of **insects** represents his struggles with courage. He is confronted with insects at key points in the novel, such as the moth in his room (p.91) when, fearing his concealment of Laura's body will be discovered, he reflects on the nature of courage; the centipede (p.126) when Ruth forces him to dig the hole in the backyard; spiders (p.173) when he and Jasper hide from a passing car; and in his final test of bravery when he confronts the insects crawling over Mad Jack's peaches (p.386). While Charlie's theft of the peaches in this scene is staged, he still needs courage to snatch them amid the 'teeming metropolis of insects' (p.386). The insects attracted to the rotting fruit also symbolise the real fear Charlie must confront: the moral corruption of the adult world that he is discovering, an idea suggested when he likens the townsfolk to wasps (p.269), a simile he also uses to express his hatred of his parents (p.101). He shares this entomophobia with Eliza, reflecting the similarity of their coming-of-age journey (p.231).

Peaches are central to a well-established test of courage in Corrigan: the 'rarest and most revered feat' (p.5) is to steal a peach from the tree on Mad Jack's property. Charlie fulfils this test in the final chapter, although the victory 'feels a little hollow' (p.389) due to its staged nature. This scene reflects Charlie's awareness of moral relativism (the idea that morality is not fixed but changes according to context). For the promise of a year free of Warwick Trent's bullying he is willing to stage the scene and reinforce Jack's undeserved reputation as crazy and dangerous.

Charlie and Jeffrey's debate about the greatest superhero reveals Charlie's internal debate over what constitutes courage. **Batman** is a symbol of courage precisely because he has the same vulnerability and fears as any other human but fights for justice regardless (p.70). Charlie comes to realise that courage lies not in grand acts of heroism, but in the simple act of recognising one's fear and persisting despite it (p.356).

Carved into both the tree in the clearing (p.200) and the side of Mad Jack's wrecked car (p.257), the word '**sorry**' becomes a significant motif throughout the novel. Initially Charlie presumes it is an 'admission of guilt' (p.200) by a murderer, but the word prompts him to reflect on morality, realising that everyone is 'buffeted between good and bad' (p.262), but that to say sorry is a gesture that recognises 'the pulse of other people's pain' (p.263). He also recognises, however, the inadequacy of apologies, both in conveying remorse and in atoning for the harm caused. Although Charlie reflects on the notion in the context of the murderers he has researched, Silvey clearly alludes to the importance of saying sorry in the Australian social context. The appearance of the word in both the 'home' in which Jasper seeks refuge from neglect and racism (p.15) and on the vehicle that killed his Aboriginal mother and effectively left him without a connection to his culture effectively directs the apology to the First Nations characters for the harm they have experienced.

The first reference to a **kite** is a simile depicting Laura's body falling when Jasper cuts her free from the tree. Later, Charlie observes some children struggling to fly a kite in the stifling air (p.104); a couple of weeks later, they 'have finally got their ragged kite going' (p.368). He reflects that the kite represents something precious – a form of freedom that people can admire even though they are confined to the ground. He uses the act of holding the string of a kite as an analogy for being possessive about someone who wants their freedom: at some point you have to be unselfish and 'cut the string' (p.369) rather than reining the kite in. The kite symbolises several of Charlie's lessons, including that:

- individual freedom is tempered by responsibility or connection to others
- people are largely motivated by self-interest
- his parents' marriage is dysfunctional, as they 'put rings on their fingers just so neither of them can leave' (p.369)
- people prefer the illusion of hope or freedom to acknowledging unpleasant realities.

The **burning Wishart house** represents the destruction of the idealised family. As shire president, with a dutiful wife and two beautiful daughters, Pete Wishart seems to represent both patriarchal and familial authority. However, the Wishart home is the site of abuse and repression of the truth about Laura's death. Its destruction can be read as the destruction of the myth of the 'perfect' family.

Narrative voice and dialogue

Charlie's love of words and reading is evident in his language choices. Words are his secret weapon, his superpower, as he enjoys debating with Jeffrey. Bullied for his sophisticated vocabulary, he feels that every new word he learns 'is like getting a punch back' (p.76). He describes Warwick Trent as having 'the cerebral finesse of an amoeba' (p.81), a fight with his mother as 'a rhetorical standoff' (p.101), and himself as 'a whirring zoetrope of half-thoughts and worries' (p.131), language unexpected of a typical thirteen-year-old. However, this is juxtaposed with his often juvenile, sarcastic and politically incorrect banter with Jeffrey, which reveals their literal childishness and brings both Charlie's philosophising and grim discoveries into stark contrast. For example, during the scene on pages 59–65, Jeffrey calls Charlie a communist, self-deprecatingly mocks his own accent, and takes advantage of the fact that his mother doesn't understand English swear words to be vulgar.

Dialogue is also used to characterise the rest of the characters. Ruth's dialogue is frequently harsh, aggressive and critical, such as when she refuses to give Charlie a reason as to why he must stay close to home, instead saying, 'Are you going to continue to backchat me, or are you going to do what you're *bloody* told?' (p.101), or when she orders him to dig a hole: 'If you do not, you'll spend the rest of this summer in your bedroom, wasps or no wasps. Do you understand?' (pp.124–5). On the other hand, Wesley is calm and gentle. Following the fight with Ruth, he tells Charlie, 'Listen, she just wants to feel as though she's respected ... if you still have a problem with something, there are smarter ways around it. You just have to be a bit more canny, okay? Diplomatic' (p.137). Jasper's dialogue reveals a thoughtful and sensitive soul at odds with his reputation, although at times he is coarse and aggressive, particularly in his emotional confrontation with Jack (pp.302–9). For example, he tells Charlie, 'that's what I reckon God really is, Charlie. It's that part inside me that's stronger and harder than anything else. And I reckon prayer is just trustin in it, havin faith in it, just askin meself to be tough' (p.196).

Dialogue also establishes the historical context, with homophobic and racist slurs that would be unacceptable today used casually by many characters, including Jeffrey, who frequently uses the word 'queer' to bait Charlie, and the men who attack An Lu referring to him as a 'red rat' (p.267).

CHAPTER-BY-CHAPTER ANALYSIS

Chapter 1 (pp.1–52)

Summary: *Jasper Jones comes to Charlie's window; Charlie follows him to a clearing in the bush outside of town and is confronted with the hanged Laura Wishart; Charlie agrees to help hide the body, although sickened by his participation.*

The opening chapter establishes the novel's bildungsroman genre, with a rather innocent Charlie beginning his journey of development, his graceless exit through the bedroom window represented metaphorically as the birth of a foal (p.2). Sneaking out of the 'womb' of his room (p.3) is Charlie's first transgression against his parents' authority. Other evidence of his juvenility includes his 'pansy sandals' (p.32) – a source of shame; that he is flattered by Jasper's attention; his awkwardness when offered a cigarette; his inability to hold his liquor; and his faith in adult authority, evident in his desire to go to the police. The symbol of peaches is introduced early in this chapter (p.5), when Charlie explains that stealing them from Mad Jack Lionel's tree is the children's yardstick for bravery.

Corrigan is established as an insular, parochial, rural mining town with a working-class population, meaning there 'isn't much class divide' (p.8). Charlie is marginalised as the town's 'social currency is sport', which he is 'lousy at' (p.8), and his academic ability, advanced vocabulary and love of literature mark him as different.

Initially excited to accompany Jasper, Charlie's world is upended when he is confronted with the body of Laura Wishart. Depicted in grim, Gothic detail, Laura's corpse becomes a symbol for the death of childhood innocence as Charlie struggles to comprehend who could murder a young girl. He is revolted by the process of moving Laura's body, thinking, 'We are monsters' (p.40). The motif of a shaken snowdome is first employed here, as everything that was 'steady and sure and sturdy' in Charlie's world has been 'shaken out of place' (p.30). The eerie, sinister clearing becomes a site of revelation, where Charlie learns truths that figure significantly in his journey to maturation.

This chapter also establishes the central mystery of the novel: who killed Laura? Jasper speculates that it is local recluse Mad Jack Lionel, and begs for Charlie's help in proving it. He has sought out Charlie because, on some level, he knows Charlie to be wise, honourable and loyal. This plays to Charlie's juvenile ego, and he sees himself as an Atticus Finch figure, initiating the novel's frequent intertextual references to Harper Lee's *To Kill a Mockingbird* (p.23).

Jasper's story of neglect and abuse at the hands of his father further unsettles Charlie, and foreshadows the fact that Laura will also be revealed as a victim of abuse at the hands of her father. Jasper's stereotyping as 'a Thief, a Liar, a Thug, a Truant' (p.6) and his history as a scapegoat for the town reveal to Charlie the awful reality that traditional authority figures, such as parents and the police, can be morally corrupt. His friendship with Jeffrey Lu, who is 'ruthlessly bullied and belted about' (p.9) for his Vietnamese heritage, has already alerted Charlie to the racism in Corrigan, but Jasper's experience reveals its entrenched nature and Charlie realises that it will inevitably result in Jasper being blamed for Laura's death.

Key point

A misfit due to his academic ability and lack of sporting prowess, Charlie is drawn to other outcasts. Both Jeffrey and Jasper are ostracised because of racism.

As Charlie and Jasper bond, Jasper reveals how a childhood of abuse and neglect forced him to grow up quickly. Charlie tries some of the stereotypical markers of adult masculinity – smoking and drinking alcohol – which merely make him ill. Although seemingly more accustomed to these activities, Jasper also vomits, suggesting that neither boy is quite the man he is desperately trying to be.

Q How does the portrait of Jasper's childhood contribute to our understanding of his motives for investigating Laura's death himself?

Q How does Silvey use imagery to reveal Charlie's inner turmoil?

Q How does the cyclical nature of this chapter, beginning with Charlie leaving his bedroom and closing with his return to it, draw attention to the changes the night's events have wrought within him?

Key vocabulary

Portentous: of momentous or awesome significance.

Transgression: an act that goes against established rules or codes of conduct.

Chapter 2 (pp.53–98)

Summary: *Charlie awakes and half expects his parents to notice how altered he is; he and Jeffrey discuss the relative merits of Superman and Batman as the archetypal superhero; he accompanies Jeffrey to cricket practice, witnessing casual racism and homophobic bullying; his crush on Eliza Wishart is revealed.*

As someone who refers to his words as 'gems' and his own stories and poems as 'jewels' (p.76), and who reflects on the wise words of Mark Twain, it is not surprising that Charlie is closer to his literature-teacher father, with whom he shares a love of writing and American (Southern Gothic) writers, than to his mother, who doesn't seem to understand him. Charlie will test his relationship with both parents, as is normal for an adolescent developing towards independence.

Key point

Charlie begins to question his black-and-white understanding of honesty, recognising that even his parents – whom he sees as good people – tell lies. In contrast, he believes Jasper Jones 'speaks the whole truth in a town of liars' (p.56).

This chapter develops the character of Jeffrey. Charlie and Jeffrey's relationship is built on their shared status as outsiders, their often vulgar banter and a shared interest in pop culture. Their debate about the relative merits of superheroes, while amusing, also reveals the kernel of Charlie's future insight into the nature of courage, as he argues that Batman is a greater superhero because he is mortal, and therefore puts himself at genuine risk as he overcomes his fears to help others.

The racism in Corrigan, and in Australia generally, is exposed as Charlie acknowledges that Jeffrey's Vietnamese heritage will prevent his talent for cricket being recognised. Later, Charlie reflects on the writing of Mark Twain in *Pudd'nhead Wilson*, noting that 'courage is resistance to fear' (p.92). He decides that Jeffrey is perhaps the bravest of them all, as he remains persistently optimistic despite his marginal position in society.

Warwick Trent, the town bully, makes his first appearance in this chapter. Warwick represents all that is valued by the town, such as athleticism and aggressive masculinity, as well as its small-mindedness, and is the antithesis of Charlie. Their interactions reveal Charlie's underlying strength of character, which will later come to the fore. Although bullied by Warwick and his mates, Charlie continues to use the vocabulary they mock, in a gesture of defiance.

Q What does Charlie's daydream about calling out others' racism (pp.80–1) reveal about his own social status?

Q What role does Charlie's insect phobia play in developing the theme of courage?

Key vocabulary

Amoeba: a primitive, one-celled organism.

Archaic: very old or old-fashioned.

Cerebral: intellectual.

Luddite: someone who is resistant to new technologies.

Chapter 3 (pp.99–144)

Summary: *Laura's disappearance puts the town on edge; Charlie begins researching true crime; he meets Eliza outside the bookstore; his mother makes him dig a hole in the backyard and fill it in again; he reflects on his parents' marriage.*

The impact of Laura's disappearance begins to permeate the town, with Charlie's mother – like other parents – requesting that he stay within sight of the house. Charlie's defiance of this is another example of him testing the boundaries of parental authority – a key aspect of his journey towards independence. Momentarily, he hates both parents: 'my father for being bewildered and useless, my mother for flying the red flag' (p.101) of absolute authority. It is ironic that Charlie both admires and resents his father for not conforming to the stereotype of masculinity, a stereotype that Charlie himself both criticises and attempts to emulate when he is with Jasper.

Charlie's library research of murder cases forces him to confront the human capacity for evil. He realises that there is often no discernible reason for such acts of cruelty. He investigates the famous cases of Eric Edgar Cooke, the 'Nedlands Monster', who murdered several people in a killing spree that many say caused Perth to lose its innocence in 'a fever of panic' (p.106), and Sylvia Likens (p.109), a young girl tortured to death by her guardian, Gertrude Baniszewski.

Charlie notes that Cooke had a cleft palate and experienced abuse as a child, and wonders whether being victimised as a child is what creates a murderer or whether everyone has within them the capacity for cruelty, and it is just 'a matter of friction and pressure' (p.108) that causes it to manifest. Cooke states he killed simply because he wanted to hurt somebody (p.108), a reason that Charlie cannot accept. From the Likens case, he realises that silence can be complicity, as Sylvia's sister Jenny and many neighbours were aware of the abuse but 'let it happen' (p.112). His research leaves him 'angry and bewildered' (p.113). Meeting Eliza on the street creates a moral dilemma for Charlie, as he decides to stay silent about Laura, which makes him 'feel like such a phoney' (p.119), wishing he could erase his knowledge. This experience characterises his ongoing struggle with his own sense of guilt and innocence.

Charlie is punished by his mother for disobeying instructions to remain close to home. She forces him to dig a large hole in the backyard, then fill it in by hand – a particularly vindictive punishment as she knows he is afraid of insects. Ruth is characterised as petty, while Charlie's reflection on her past suggests he at least tries to understand her. He appreciates that Ruth is desperately unhappy – with her loveless marriage, her small-town life and her grief at the loss of a baby daughter – and that, while his father has his writing, she has little joy in her life. The hole is an important symbol, emphasising the pointless cruelty of some people, as well as foreshadowing the 'holes' that Ruth digs for herself through her choices in life.

In this chapter we also come to learn that even good people can keep secrets. Not only is Charlie harbouring his own secret, but he also suspects his father is privately writing a novel, something Charlie desperately wishes to be privy to but is excluded from.

Q How does the plot of *Breakfast at Tiffany's* mirror the romantic vision Charlie constructs of his fantasy relationship with Eliza?

Q Why does Eliza's ability to casually lie to her mother unsettle Charlie?

Q How does the insight into Ruth's background and the loss of her child contrast with Charlie's critical representation of her?

Key vocabulary

Caricature: an exaggerated portrait.

Macabre: disturbing, gruesome, usually due to a focus on crime or death.

Rapacious: greedy or grasping.

Repartee: quick, witty comments or replies.

Chapter 4 (pp.145–63)

Summary: *Jeffrey's relatives are killed in Vietnam; Charlie reflects on the human capacity for violence, whether dropping bombs on civilians, killing young girls, or beating up someone because of their vocabulary; he discusses Laura's disappearance with his father.*

Charlie makes a somewhat disturbing self-discovery. He has already hidden his involvement in Laura's disappearance from his parents; now he must also conceal it from Jeffrey, his best friend, a true indicator of his evolving morality and his own capacity for deception (p.146).

The grim reality of the Vietnam War is exposed here, with Jeffrey receiving news of his relatives being killed. Charlie asks if Mr and Mrs Lu will visit Vietnam and Jeffrey's startled reply, 'there are *bombs*, Chuck. It's a war' (p.152) reveals that Charlie is still quite naive, despite his recent experiences. The two boys debate the merits of knowing when one might die, in a manner that demonstrates their childish banter but also an existential curiosity beyond their years. Charlie continues to struggle with notions of morality, as he later realises that he would not be as affected by the bombing of Vietnamese civilians were it not for his friendship with Jeffrey, a realisation he connects with Corrigan's parochialism; it is 'a town of barnacles' who 'clench themselves shut and choose not to know about dying' (p.161).

Charlie's conversation with his parents regarding Laura's disappearance is another important step in his journey to adulthood. While Ruth does not wish to discuss the situation, Wesley agrees to talk to Charlie, a subtle recognition that his son can no longer be sheltered from the harsh realities of life. Charlie's reflections on Laura's death, the Vietnam War, violence suffered by children and the racism experienced by his friends make him question the nature of the world, and the role of hope – however false – as a way to 'seek solace' (p.162) amid the gloom. He still believes, however, that truth is better than hope and knowing is better than not knowing, which he sees as a kind of purgatorial existence.

Q What does Charlie's conclusion that truth is better than hope reveal about his struggle to carry the secret of Laura's death?

Q How does Silvey use metaphors in this chapter to reinforce Charlie's unsettled state?

Key vocabulary

Verbosity: using more words than needed.

Chapter 5 (pp.164–207)

Summary: *Mrs Lu is attacked; Jasper reveals he has been beaten and locked up by the police, with Pete Wishart's support; Jasper suspects Mad Jack Lionel is responsible for Laura's death, and feels guilty for failing to protect her; Charlie discovers the word 'sorry' carved into a tree; Charlie's absence is discovered; confronted by Ruth's fear, Charlie breaks down in tears, vowing to leave Corrigan.*

At the town meeting, Charlie is forced to recognise the impact of his own silence regarding Laura's death. It contributes to his sense of otherness, as if he is 'made of different stuff' or 'from a different place' (p.166). This conflict is exacerbated when he is confronted with the town's racism after Sue Findlay abuses Mrs Lu and throws scalding tea over her, which he finds incomprehensible. Sue is upset that her son has been conscripted into supporting the war in Vietnam, in which her husband has already been killed, and, like other Australians at the time, she ignorantly blames Vietnamese immigrants.

Key point

This is an important milestone in Charlie's development. In questioning why no one helped Mrs Lu, he realises once more the complicity of silence, as in the case of Sylvia Likens. The realisation that those who stand by and do nothing are as culpable as the assailants makes him more determined to help clear Jasper's name.

Charlie's second outing with Jasper sees him once again experimenting with the markers of masculine adulthood, as they share a bottle of whiskey. Charlie's ability to drink it without vomiting – at least initially – symbolises his steps towards maturity. When he does vomit, it is after he has drunk water from the very dam where they have hidden Laura, symbolic of the way in which the secrets he keeps are sickening him. However, hearing that the police, along with Pete Wishart, were responsible for beating and incarcerating Jasper shakes Charlie's faith in adult authorities even further, so that his 'head is spinning' (p.179) in an echo of his first traumatic confrontation with corruption in Chapter 1.

The discussion of Jasper's skill at poker symbolises the recurring theme of deception, as Jasper's poker face is merely a mask to hide the 'rubbish cards' (p.182) he has been dealt in life. Charlie learns more about Jasper's relationship with Laura and his suspicions that Mad Jack Lionel is the culprit, something that Charlie, with his empathy for the outsider, is not quite ready to believe; 'pinning it all on the town recluse with the shady history' seems 'too convenient' (p.189). Jasper explains that he went away without telling Laura, setting the scene for the later revelation that this played a tragic role in Laura taking her life, which complicates notions of innocence and guilt. His guilt, Jasper reveals, is because he had a duty to protect Laura (p.189): from what, he refrains from disclosing. Charlie is frustrated that Jasper is withholding information from him: he is still being treated as a child. Everybody, it seems, has secrets – even Jasper, whom he believed was the only truthful person in Corrigan.

The boys' discussion of solipsism (self-centredness) is significant. Not only does it emphasise Charlie's philosophical bent, it also reveals Jasper's intelligence and sensitivity, in stark contrast to the townsfolk's stereotypical assumptions about him. Such discussion is central to the bildungsroman genre, in which the adolescent protagonist shifts from a solipsistic view of the world to realising that they are a part of a greater whole, society: 'a small cog in a bigger engine' (p.192), as Jasper puts it. The questioning of belief systems, with their 'holes and gaps and slippery bits' (p.191), is also characteristic of bildungsromane protagonists, who wrestle with their moral code on their journey to adulthood.

Q What comparisons can you draw between Charlie's and Jasper's respective journeys towards maturity at this point?

Chapter 6 (pp.208–77)

Summary: *Charlie is confined to his bedroom; he recounts his skilful lying to protect Jasper; Ruth argues with Wesley; Charlie and Eliza flirt as they watch Jeffrey play cricket; Charlie recounts another visit from Jasper; they discover the word 'sorry' scratched into the side of Mad Jack's car and interpret it as a sign of guilt; An Lu is attacked.*

Charlie's night-time excursion with Jasper reveals his new-found capacity for duplicity as, caught out, he lies to both his parents and the police to avoid implicating Jasper. Like the genial police officer who is really a 'monster' (p.211), Charlie manipulates appearances, though, in his case, it is to protect Jasper and also himself, given that he is 'partly responsible' (p.211) for covering up Laura's death.

Charlie continues to gain insights into his parents' relationship. During their argument, Wesley once again stays silent rather than engaging in conflict, in stark contrast to Ruth becoming 'hysterical … blaming Corrigan for everything' (p.213) and turning on her husband, questioning 'what sort of *man* he thought he was' (p.212) and accusing him of being remote and disengaged. His only response is that there are 'things' that he knows (p.213), probably alluding to Ruth's affair, which is revealed later.

Grounded, Charlie reads, writes obsessively and imagines a future with Eliza in which he is a successful author, recognised by Ernest Hemingway and dancing with Eliza in a Manhattan ballroom. These daydreams reflect Charlie's still-naive perspective. Literature is his escape, in contrast to Ruth and Jasper's very practical desire to leave Corrigan.

In a rare moment of genuine joy, Jeffrey is finally given the opportunity to play for the Corrigan cricket team and subsequently wins the match for them. He is initially unimpressive, dropping a catch and prompting racist abuse from Warwick Trent. However, as Jeffrey remains positive and focused and begins to score runs, the attitude of the team shifts to one of 'grudging respect' (p.237) then to support (p.249) then outright 'congratulation' of the 'hero' (p.242). Jeffrey's sporting prowess meets Corrigan's standards for social acceptance.

Charlie's relationship with Eliza develops, although it is still at a stage of awkward flirtation. Their conversation is interrupted when Eliza bursts into tears, a response Charlie assumes is due to grief but which, as we learn later, is also tinged with guilt, suggested by her admission that she 'know[s] things' and is 'not a good person' (p.230). It forces Charlie to confront his own role in Laura's disappearance, and his dishonesty in pursuing Eliza while keeping this terrible secret. Despite this, when Eliza indicates her interest in Charlie, they kiss for the first time, a significant rite of passage that Charlie describes as both 'weird and nice' (p.246).

Jeffrey's teasing about kissing a girl, the conversation about penis-fingers, spider-hats and superheros, and Charlie's self-satisfaction at kissing Eliza remind the reader that, despite the horrifying circumstances in which they are embroiled, they are still young and deserve to be innocent.

Important in this chapter is Charlie's reflection on the word 'sorry'. He realises that all people are 'buffeted between good and bad' but that good people 'can tell the difference' (p.262). His empathy is revealed in his remark that 'sorry means you feel the pulse of other people's pain, as well as your own' (p.263). However, he recognises that an apology is also self-serving, intended to make the speaker feel better, and is largely inadequate for reparation. Silvey clearly draws parallels here with the political discourse surrounding reconciliation with Australia's First Nations peoples.

The scene in which An Lu is attacked and his garden destroyed is a violent reminder of the precarity of the Lu family's position in the town. Coming so soon after Jeffrey's seeming acceptance by the cricket team, it reveals how fragile that acceptance is, and that xenophobia remains ingrained. Indicating that the town, like its youthful characters, might be growing up, several men, including Wesley, rush to An's defence. As Charlie has resented his father's passivity, this is a redemptive moment for Wesley, and the more cheerful game of cards that the Bucktin family plays afterwards suggests a renewal of their relationship, although Charlie questions his parents' ability to 'distance themselves from what just happened out there so easily' (p.275).

Q How does this chapter reveal Charlie's growth towards an adult understanding of the world?

Key vocabulary

Belle: a beautiful girl or woman.

En masse: in a group or all together (French).

Galvanising: inspiring or shocking into action.

Hackneyed: being unoriginal or clichéd.

Menial: low-status or demeaning.

Nonplussed: surprised or confused as to how to act.

Obstreperous: noisy and difficult to control.

Philistine: a person hostile or indifferent to the arts.

Purgatory: a place where souls are punished and purified before being admitted to Heaven.

Torrid: hot and dry; passionate.

Chapter 7 (pp.278–369)

Summary: *Charlie feels guilty at the thought of leaving Jeffrey behind if he escapes Corrigan; he fantasises about a life of freedom on the road with Jasper; Wesley reveals he has been writing a novel; Jasper and Charlie confront Mad Jack and learn that he is Jasper's grandfather, and responsible for the death of Jasper's mother in a car accident; Eliza comes to Charlie's window and leads him to the clearing; they discover Ruth being intimate with another man in a car; Eliza relates the story of Laura's abuse, pregnancy and ultimate suicide; Jasper arrives and is overcome with grief; the three fantasise about leaving Corrigan together; the Sarge takes Eliza to the police station.*

Chapter 7 is the novel's climax and includes a series of tests of Charlie's character and shocking revelations that lead to an adult understanding of the world. Charlie's courage is tested by Jasper's plea to confront Mad Jack Lionel; his loyalty is tested when he is tempted to spend the evening with Eliza instead; and his integrity is tested by Eliza before she confesses the truth about Laura's death.

The idea that people turn a blind eye to uncomfortable truths is reinforced through Jeffrey's analysis of the mermaid myth. Rather than focusing on the creature's monstrousness, pirates focus only on the parts that are desirable, and 'squint away the fishy bits' (p.285). Charlie realises, however, that it is only a matter of time before his own 'fishy bits' – his involvement in Laura's disappearance – will come to light. This reinforces his desire to 'leave with Jasper' (p.289), reflecting both a fear of his own secrets coming to light and his loyalty to Jasper.

The confrontation with Mad Jack Lionel reveals Charlie's progress towards the courage he desires. He is deathly afraid of going to Jack's house, but does so to support Jasper, even when tormented by insects along the way. He still romanticises Jasper and allows himself to be led by the older boy, even though he realises that Jasper, too, is 'wavering' (p.300) in his self-assurance. When Jasper reverts to 'a bleating, scared, hurt kid' (p.308), Charlie feels betrayed, as his image of Jasper as mature and worldly is shattered, and he realises that Jack is not a murderer but simply a misunderstood, lonely old man. The fact that Charlie sees this before Jasper does reveals his growth towards adulthood: their roles are reversed, and Jasper's accusation of Jack seems childish.

Although Jasper appears confident and self-assured, his stereotypically masculine adult behaviours – confronting Jack, smoking, drinking, swearing – are attempts to hide his own insecurities, as empty as 'Batman's cape' (p.300). Jack's history in Corrigan, particularly the revelation that he is both Jasper's grandfather and responsible for the death of the boy's mother, reveals to Charlie the pervasive extent of the conflict between appearances and the secrets they mask. Jack's life has been clouded by 'ruthless' rumours (p.316) that have turned him into a 'pariah' (p.317). This reveals the nature of Corrigan, where appearances mask people's true characters, as evidenced by the genial police sergeant who brutalises Jasper; the respected shire president who abuses his own daughter; Ruth, whose concern with appearances contradicts her own infidelity; Eliza, whose poise masks her guilt and loneliness; and Jasper, whose own reputation is a far cry from the tragic figure he really is.

A further step in Charlie's coming of age occurs when he confronts Ruth after discovering her affair. He feels 'the balance between [them] shift' (p.323) as her compromised position undermines her parental authority. He refuses to follow her instructions, saying '*this* means I don't have to do what you say anymore' (p.324). Ruth's loss of authority is reinforced through Charlie's awareness that she looks 'like a child … scared and lost and unhappy' (p.324), and he says, 'I also feel sympathy for her'. He realises that he doesn't 'understand a thing about this world: about people, and why they do the things they do' (p.324), a continuing refrain that reiterates his inability to comprehend the complex and contradictory nature of the adult world.

In an echo of Jasper's visit, Eliza also turns up at Charlie's window, foreshadowing a second, this time climactic, revelation that will take place in the clearing, where Eliza explains the circumstances of Laura's death. The style of Charlie's narration of this, in a long, almost stream-of-consciousness-style passage, reflects how he is overwhelmed with the magnitude of what he learns and is desperate 'to get it out' (p.329).

'Sorry' is a potent motif in this chapter, with Charlie realising that Eliza carved the word into the tree in apology to her sister, and him and Eliza apologising to each other for the secrets they have kept. Their emotions, however, are complex. Charlie acknowledges Eliza's greater anguish and is quick to reassure her that Laura's death was not her fault, but he is simultaneously angry with her for keeping the letter secret, causing Jasper additional pain. Eliza, too, realises that Charlie has kept secrets from her, including the location of her sister's body. This is further evidence of Charlie's realisation that the world is not black and white, and that people's motivations are complex, often driven by hurt, fear and self-interest.

Charlie's occupation of Jasper's tree-hollow home could be read as suggesting he has metaphorically taken over Jasper's role as the most adult of the three of them, with his new understanding of the world. This is reinforced by his courage in diving into the dam to save Jasper, rescuing him from the guilt and fear that threatens to drown him.

There are clear parallels between Charlie and Eliza:

- both are shaken from childhood naivety into adult understanding after a journey into the clearing
- both initially question Jasper's role in Laura's death
- both are physically sickened by their sudden confrontation with death and corruption
- both have carried secrets and deceived others
- both are tormented by their sense of guilt.

Charlie's journey towards an adult understanding of the world is now almost complete: he sees that people are not as they seem, that even good people are fallible, and that courage is not about being without fear, but learning to 'walk with the weight' of it (p.356).

Q In what ways does Charlie's understanding of the tragedy of Laura's death shift from simple to complex?

Q How does Charlie's insight into other people's motivations affect his understanding of his own?

Key vocabulary

Assuage: to appease, soothe or satisfy.

Pariah: a despised outcast.

Serenade: music or song typically performed to attract a love interest.

Chapter 8 (pp.370–6)

Summary: *Ruth leaves Corrigan; Eliza confronts her mother regarding her sister's abuse; Charlie and Eliza's relationship deepens.*

Ruth's departure from Corrigan is an explosive scene treated in a surprisingly unemotional way by Charlie. Following the exposure of her infidelity, Ruth argues loudly with Wesley, drawing the attention of the neighbours; she tears up Wesley's manuscript and empties Charlie's writing onto the bed, perhaps jealous of this shared passion from which she is excluded. Despite this, Charlie conveys little in the way of an overtly emotional response, feeling her absence only 'because something familiar seems missing' (p.372).

Having realised the fallibility and even corruption of adults, both Charlie and Eliza choose to stand up to them: Charlie stands up to his mother over her hypocrisy; Eliza stands firm against the police, refusing to divulge any information about Laura (p.373); she also challenges the authority of her parents, offering her mother 'neither comfort nor love' (p.374) as she calmly reveals the truth behind Laura's disappearance, while not divulging the location of her body unless her mother is prepared to 'see that things were put right' (p.374).

Charlie and Eliza continue to visit Jasper's clearing, even sleeping in the tree hollow he used to call home. Instead of being a site of fear and trauma, it becomes a place of healing: Eliza talks to and brings gifts for her sister, and her relationship with Charlie develops. There are moments, however, when Eliza puts on an act, adopting what Charlie refers to as her 'Golightly voice' (p.376), in reference to a character in the novella and film *Breakfast at Tiffany's*. Along with the maintenance of secrets regarding domestic abuse in the Wishart family and the whereabouts of Laura's body, this suggests that the tension between honesty and deception is not easily resolved.

Charlie's sexual confidence grows, and he and Eliza become intimate. Charlie believes he loves her (although he is not yet prepared to say it). Again, this relationship demonstrates his increasing maturity, physically but also emotionally. Although his desire to marry Eliza may seem naively romantic, at least Charlie realises that he does not yet have 'the right words' (p.376).

Notable in this chapter is Jasper's absence, although Charlie does still refer to 'Jasper's glade' (p.376). Much like the body of Laura, Jasper remains in the clearing as a kind of haunting presence, a reminder of those children who are forever lost. Many lost children are referenced throughout the novel – Sylvia Likens, the Beaumont children and, of course, Laura Wishart – but Jasper, too, is lost, a victim of both familial and societal neglect. His disappearance is perhaps all the more tragic because it receives none of the attention given to those other, white, children.

Q Charlie does not leave Corrigan, as he once desired. What does this suggest about his new-found maturity?

Q What does the ongoing silence within the Wishart household reveal about truth and justice?

Chapter 9 (pp.377–94)

Summary: *The new school year begins; Jasper fails to return; Jeffrey is included in the cricket team; Charlie barters for freedom from bullies by contriving to 'steal' peaches from Jack's yard and is declared a hero; Eliza simply watches as the Wishart house burns and her father is attended to by paramedics.*

This final brief chapter continues to tie up loose narrative threads, revealing that Jeffrey's cricketing prowess has earned him a degree of acceptance in the town and that Jasper has indeed departed Corrigan, leaving Charlie a gift of cigarettes, alcohol and a pen. This connects with the opening chapter, where the two bonded over cigarettes and alcohol after hiding Laura's body and Charlie shared his dream of becoming a writer.

The theme of secrecy and lies is rounded out with Charlie's subterfuge with Jack. Although initially disappointed to discover that even good people sometimes lie, Charlie has learnt that morality is relative. The staging of a dramatic encounter with 'Mad' Jack secures Charlie's reputation among his peers. Despite the artifice, the act is a genuine test of courage for Charlie, as he must overcome his morbid fear of insects to collect the fruit that lies rotting under Jack's tree. It is a final rite of passage typical of the bildungsroman, success in which will grant Charlie his acceptance into society.

The final image in the novel – Eliza watching her family home burn to the ground – is significant. The implication is that it is she who set the fire, as in the previous chapter she indicated that her father would be punished (p.374) and she does not flinch when the house goes up in flames (p.392). For Eliza, the burning of the family home – not only the site of the abuse suffered by Laura but also of her parents' ongoing deception in refusing to admit it – is as much an act of catharsis as of vengeance. It is also an opportunity for Eliza to exorcise her own guilt, aware of the role her silence played in Laura's death. As Charlie notes, human motivations are rarely simple and 'there's always more to know' (p.393).

As the flames begin to die down, rumours begin that Jasper Jones is the culprit. While Jeffrey, Charlie and even Eliza have been able to find ways to exist within Corrigan, Jasper cannot, and ends the novel as marginalised as he began it.

Throughout the novel, the snowdome motif has symbolised the unsettling of Charlie's world as he realises its flaws. Here he refers to the ash-filled sky as the 'antipodean snowdome' (p.392) and in the final scene the ash settles around him and Eliza (p.394), suggesting that he has regained equilibrium. It is at this moment he finds 'the right words' (p.394) to say to Eliza – presumably that he loves her, as implied in the previous chapter.

Key vocabulary

Antipodean: relating to Australia or New Zealand.

Reconnaissance: observation to gain strategic advantage.

Q What is the symbolic relationship between the burning of the Wishart house and the power of young people to seek justice?

CHARACTERS & RELATIONSHIPS

Charlie Bucktin

Key quotes

'I'm lousy at sport, and better than most at school, which garners me only ire in the classroom and resentment when report cards are issued.' (pp.8–9)

'Because you're smart, and you're different to the others, and I thought you'd understand, for sure.' (Jasper, p.28)

'I bruise like a peach. And I'm afraid of insects. And I don't know how to fight.' (p.92)

Charlie begins the novel as a naive and somewhat childish thirteen-year-old. Ostracised by his peers due to his sophisticated vocabulary and academic aptitude, Charlie feels drawn to other outsiders, such as Jeffrey and Jasper. He recognises that both are bullied due to their ethnicity, but initially feels powerless to intervene.

The insularity of Charlie's world is shattered when he is confronted with the body of Laura Wishart, and the realisation that true evil exists. Through researching perpetrators of murder and cruelty, and his later awareness of the abuse that led to Laura's suicide, Charlie tries to comprehend why people are driven to commit such acts. He wonders if such people are products of their own traumatic childhoods or whether all humans have the capacity for evil, and struggles with the possibility that such events are simply beyond reason.

A voracious reader, Charlie takes life lessons from his favourite authors, and idolises his father, a literature teacher and, later, author. He uses writing as a form of catharsis and there are metafictional suggestions that *Jasper Jones* is Charlie's own novel, an attempt to make sense of the events of an extraordinary summer. Literature is also a means of escape, and he fantasises about being a respected author, receiving affirmation from his favourite writers. He romanticises Jasper as the rebellious outsider, and imagines them being on a literary road trip together.

As expected in a bildungsroman, Charlie tests the boundaries of authority. He challenges his parents, initially in the way many adolescents would: sneaking out, answering back, disobeying their instructions. But his resistance escalates to maintaining his silence about Laura's disappearance, lying to the police and rejecting his mother. He experiences moral conflict, torn between his loyalties to Jasper, Jeffrey and Eliza, and guilt due to his involvement in hiding Laura's body. His relationship with Eliza represents the fulfilment of another rite of passage.

Key point

Charlie gains an adult understanding of the cruel nature of the world, learning that adults can be deceptive and morally corrupt, the realities of death and grief, the systemic nature of racism and bigotry, the impact of war and the potential meaninglessness of life.

Perhaps the most important lesson Charlie learns is about courage, which he defines as learning to live with one's fears. But his insights into the nature of courage are externalised: he admires it in Jasper, Jeffrey and Eliza. Despite his criticism of those who turn a blind eye to injustice – such as Sylvia Likens' neighbours, those who failed to assist Mrs Lu, and even his own father failing to stand up to Ruth – Charlie demonstrates little evidence of standing up to injustice himself.

Q To what extent does Charlie come to embody the courage and perseverance he so admires in others, such as Jasper and Jeffrey?

Jasper Jones

Key quotes

'Jasper Jones has a terrible reputation in Corrigan. He's a Thief, a Liar, a Thug, a Truant. He's lazy and unreliable. He's a feral and an orphan, or as good as. His mother is dead and his father is no good.' (pp.6–7)

'And Jasper Jones sounds like a child. Like a bleating, scared, hurt kid.' (p.308)

'He's too smart and too fast for them. He's too clever and canny.' (p.394)

A year older than Charlie, Jasper presents as worldly and street smart but, as Charlie later comes to realise, his self-assurance is a facade and Jasper is as lonely, fearful and flawed as the other characters. Indeed, this is why he seeks Charlie's assistance in solving the mystery surrounding Laura's death, needing both an adviser and a friend. Having lost his mother and been raised by an alcoholic father, Jasper has learned to be self-reliant, occasionally resorting to crime to support himself in the face of his father's neglect. Tragically, Rosie's death has meant that Jasper has grown up with no connection to his mother's culture or his extended family, namely Mad Jack Lionel, Jasper's paternal grandfather.

Despite his lack of formal education, Jasper is philosophical, discussing with Charlie his perspective on belief systems, specifically that faith in a higher power is simply a fear of taking responsibility for oneself. In light of this, he feels intensely guilty about Laura's death, believing that his relationship with her conferred a duty to protect her. His misguided attempts to unmask her killer reflect both his lack of faith in the police system that has brutalised him and a desire to expiate his guilt for failing Laura.

Despite his prowess as a footballer, Jasper is marginalised by Corrigan, stereotyped as a troublemaker and scapegoated for every crime and misdemeanour. He seeks escape by retreating to the clearing he has claimed in the bush outside of town, the same clearing in which Laura hangs herself.

Key point

Despite the friendship of Charlie and, more grudgingly, Eliza, Jasper remains marginalised and, in the novel's resolution, he simply slips away, knowing that he will remain a constant victim of Corrigan's culture of prejudice and suspicion.

Q What, if any, parallels can be drawn between Jasper's experiences in Corrigan and the historical experiences of First Nations people in Australia?

Jeffrey Lu

Key quotes

'Jeffrey is unflappable. He has a smile that you can't wipe or slap or goad off his face. And unlike me, he never stoops to sycophancy or spite. In a way, he's more assured than any of those vindictive bastards with peach pits in their pockets.' (p.9)

'In this frightened town, Jeffrey Lu, its shortest, slightest occupant, is fearless.' (p.238)

Jeffrey is Charlie's humorous and intelligent twelve-year-old best friend, an outstanding cricketer whose Vietnamese heritage makes him another victim of the town's bigotry. Like Jasper, Jeffrey is violently bullied, and the cricket team marginalises him despite his obvious skill. However, whereas Charlie expresses fear and self-doubt, Jeffrey displays a dogged perseverance and remarkable resilience. He is cheerful and optimistic and persists with cricket until he finally proves his value so spectacularly that he is granted a degree of acceptance in sport-loving Corrigan. This determination leads Charlie to characterise Jeffrey as the bravest person he knows.

Jeffrey uses vulgar and self-deprecating humour, often exaggerating his accent or stereotypes arising from his Vietnamese heritage. While this is part of his adolescent banter, the implication is that such humour is a coping mechanism, a mask in the same vein as Jasper's nonchalance.

Jeffrey's frequent use of 'queer' as a playful insult to Charlie, the homophobic nature of some of the bullying he receives and his teasing jealousy of Charlie's relationship with Eliza have led to inferences that Jeffrey has a romantic interest in Charlie. They are drawn together by their status as outsiders but Charlie's loyalty to Jeffrey is tested when his relationships with Jasper and Eliza develop and oblige him to keep secrets from his best friend.

Eliza Wishart

Key quotes

'Eliza's manner has always intrigued me. She seems troubled, yet infinitely untroubled.' (p.71)

'I sat and just watched it happen because I was scared. I killed her, Charlie.' (p.347)

'But I also have a suspicion that Eliza might be less concerned with what's right, less concerned about uncovering the truth, than she is about ensuring that she and Jasper Jones, and maybe her father too, are meted out the penance that she feels they each deserve.' (p.361)

Charlie's love interest, Eliza is beautiful, intelligent and poised. Like all in the Wishart family, she maintains a facade: her articulateness and measured nature mask her guilt over not preventing Laura's suicide. Charlie first suspects that Eliza knows more than she is saying because she seems too calm and assured, and he notes a curious affected quality to her voice, as if she is playing the character of Holly Golightly from *Breakfast at Tiffany's*. The extent of Eliza's feeling of guilt is shown in the novel's climax, when she divulges her powerlessness to stop either the abuse within her family home or its devastating consequences, and Charlie realises that she carved the mysterious 'sorry' into the tree trunk.

Despite the fact that Charlie has kept secrets from her, his feelings for her are tested when he discovers that Eliza has been withholding information from him – namely that she knew the truth about her sister's death from the beginning – and when she continues to blame Jasper for letting Laura down. They are able to overcome this and, with the three of them intending to run away from Corrigan together, it is clear that Eliza also forgives Jasper, recognising his genuine love and grief for Laura.

Eliza reveals a strength of character – and no small degree of vengeance – in the novel's resolution. Despite the cajoling and threats of the police, she refuses to disclose any knowledge of Laura's fate, holds her mother to account for staying silent and, ultimately, it is implied that she burns down her family home with her father still in it.

Q It is implied that Eliza sets fire to the family home. Does this demonstrate her agency, in punishing her parents for their silence, or do you see it as a destructive act that perpetuates a culture of violence?

Wesley Bucktin

Key quotes

'My father is a serene and reasonable man, but those words had him snapping his cutlery down and glaring at me through his thick blackrimmed glasses.' (p.7)
'My father is infuriating, but he's a good and honest person.' (pp.129–30)
'Why does he have to be so sensible? Why does have to phrase things so well? He should have been a lawyer, like Atticus Finch. But he'd have to stand up for something then.' (p.136)

Mild-mannered literature teacher Wesley is idolised by his son. Charlie is thrilled when Wesley allows him access to his library, sharing his favourite writers with his son, and when, against Ruth's wishes, Wesley agrees to talk to Charlie about Laura's disappearance, realising his son is no longer a child. Charlie imagines his father as Atticus Finch, the wise and principled lawyer from *To Kill a Mockingbird*. When he discovers his father has been secretly writing a novel of his own, Charlie feels betrayed because Wes didn't share this with him, but when he puts these feelings aside and reads the manuscript he is immensely proud of his father.

Charlie's opinion of his father changes over the course of the novel. He becomes frustrated by what he sees as his father's passivity, particularly when it comes to his relationship with Ruth. Charlie feels that his father allows his wife to belittle him, and sees his refusal to rise to her provocation as weakness. This changes when Wes comes to the aid of An Lu, ordering his attackers to go home, a phrase Charlie echoes when he finds his mother in the arms of another man. When Ruth leaves Corrigan, Charlie reverses his earlier opinion of his father's passivity, rationalising it as strategic rather than weak. Father and son embark on a new home routine together, happily adapting to life without Ruth.

Q Research the character of Atticus Finch. What parallels do you see between his character and that of Wesley Bucktin?

Ruth Bucktin

Key quotes

'My mother has become so hard. It's perplexing. She's always been curt and impatient, but there used to be warmth beneath it all.' (p.127)

'She looks like a child. Scared and lost and unhappy.' (p.324)

Focalised through Charlie's perspective, Ruth Bucktin is characterised as petty, mean and vindictive. She lashes out at Charlie and is particularly cruel in making him dig an enormous hole in the backyard then fill it in again with his hands. She berates her husband, Wesley, accusing him of being cold and distant. She has an affair, and ultimately leaves Corrigan after imploding spectacularly, abandoning her husband and son.

A kinder reading would acknowledge that Ruth is grieving the loss of her baby daughter, feels trapped in a loveless marriage with a man she married in haste, and is excluded from the close relationship her husband and son share. Coming from a privileged background, Ruth has struggled to adapt to Corrigan life, something Charlie acknowledges, noting that his father at least has an outlet in his writing.

When Charlie discovers Ruth and her lover, the power dynamic shifts between them, with Charlie stating he will not listen to her any further and ordering her home instead. With this final straw, Ruth seems to break and is depicted as childlike. In a final, self-destructive argument, she shatters the facade of respectability she has maintained by destroying Wesley's manuscript, and very publicly leaves town.

Q To what extent does Silvey's choice of Charlie as first-person narrator shape our understanding of Ruth as a wife, mother and woman?

Mad Jack Lionel

Key quotes

'Mad Jack Lionel isn't a criminal. He's probably not even mad. He's just old and sad and poor and lonely.' (pp.308–9)

'And Jack Lionel's portrait was smudged with ink and smeared in shit, and he made no effort to wipe it clean. And so he became the monster and the killer that they all said he was. A low man, a madman. A pariah.' (pp.316–17)

Mad Jack Lionel is the town's mysterious recluse, akin to Boo Radley in *To Kill a Mockingbird*. Jack is suspected to have murdered a woman, a myth that has become so entrenched in Corrigan that to steal a peach from the tree near his front door is considered the ultimate test of bravery. When he is finally confronted by Jasper and Charlie, who suspect Jack murdered Laura, the tragic truth is revealed: Jack is Jasper's grandfather, and the woman he killed in a car accident was Jasper's mother, whom he was taking to hospital. Grief and guilt turned him into a recluse and, as rumours spread, he retreated from society altogether.

Jack's story illustrates the power of prejudice and innuendo to shape people's perceptions, and suggests that the truth is often hidden behind false facades. Rather than a murderer or madman, Jack is simply a sad and lonely old man, guilt-ridden but desperate to make amends to his grandson. Although he and Jasper reconcile once the facts are revealed, it is too late to provide Jasper with the security that might have prevented his leaving. Jack does, however, support Charlie by participating in the subterfuge to help him successfully 'steal' the peaches, even increasing the dramatic value by allowing himself to be pushed over by Charlie, strengthening the boy's credibility among his peers.

Q Jack seems to be at the crux of many of the novel's themes. What is his significance in the lessons Charlie learns?

THEMES, IDEAS & VALUES

Honesty and deception

Key quotes

'See, most people you meet, they'll talk you through fifty layers of gauze and tinting.' (p.55)

'Nobody is truly virtuous, nobody avoids the creeping curse. Every character in every story is buffeted between good and bad, between right and wrong. But it's good people who can tell the difference, who know when they've crossed the line.' (p.262)

Corrigan is a town in which appearances mask a seedy underbelly of deception and corruption. Charlie has 'niggling doubts' about people's honesty, feeling that Corrigan is 'a town of liars', and that his perceptions of Jasper, in particular, are marred by the 'foggy community fibs' that circulate within it (p.56). This disturbs Charlie, and he agrees to investigate Laura's death to reveal the truth and exonerate Jasper. Secrets make him uncomfortable: he resents his father for keeping his novel-writing a secret, and is extremely anxious about staying quiet about his role in Laura's disappearance.

The more Charlie understands the adult world, the more dishonest he realises it is. In a somewhat cynical life lesson, he chooses not to become a champion of truth and honesty, and instead perpetuates his own dishonesty in order to survive. In fact, he discovers he has a 'gift for lies' (p.209). He and Eliza maintain the secret of Laura's whereabouts; he lies to both his parents and the police; and he carefully stage-manages his apparent 'theft' of Jack Lionel's peaches to gain status within the town and earn himself a year free of bullying.

Throughout the novel, many secrets come to light – Ruth's affair, Wesley's novel, Jasper's mother's fate, Jack Lionel's identity, the truth about Laura's death, the abuse within the Wishart household – but these are not necessarily made public. Instead, like Laura's body, some truths remain forever hidden from view. Silvey seems to suggest that secrets and lies are an inevitable part of life and to endorse the notion of moral relativism: whether a lie is immoral or not depends on the reason for it. As he is driven by a desire to protect Jasper, whom he knows will inevitably suffer for Laura's death, as well as by his realisation that the authorities in whom he is supposed to trust are corrupt, Charlie's dishonesty is made acceptable to the reader. What he learns as he matures is that the truth rarely triumphs in this society and to compromise it is sometimes necessary.

Appearances versus reality

Key quotes

'But ... But he's the shire president.' (p.179)

'Maybe that's why this town is so content to face in on itself, to keep everything so settled and smooth and serene.' (p.312)

Charlie is confronted at many points with carefully constructed facades. Most notable is Jasper's revelation that the local police are racist and brutal, locking Jasper up without evidence and beating him (pp.177–8). Charlie is incredulous, but later notes that the comforting and paternal policeman is the same 'monster' who gave Jasper cigarette burns (p.211). In the shocking climax, he learns that Pete Wishart, the shire president, is capable not only of racist violence against Jasper, but also the physical and sexual abuse of his daughter. The authorities in Corrigan are, in fact, its worst villains.

A further example of deceptive appearances is, of course, the facade that Ruth constructs for herself, which, following the discovery of her affair and her departure from Corrigan, is shattered. The 'careful varnish' Ruth has painted over her life is stripped away and her 'ugly and loud and mean' self is revealed (p.370), not only to Charlie but also to the neighbours.

Good lies and strategic silence

Key quotes

'I discovered a gift for lies. I looked straight at them and offered up the best story I could muster.' (p.209)
'Of course, I'm asking her to lie. I'm asking her to pull a blanket over parts of this story. To comb it over, to change its colour and complexion.' (p.361)

Not all lies are inherently evil, as Charlie comes to discover. He knows that his parents are dishonest, lying about things 'that don't even matter', such as his dad's comb-over hairstyle (p.55) or his mother telling her sisters she loves living in Corrigan (p.55). He believes that the older people get, 'the more brazen and desperate' the lies become (p.55). He reflects on why people lie, and particularly why his parents are dishonest about their relationship. It is partly because they are trying to protect Charlie's innocence, as is also revealed when Ruth refuses to discuss Laura's disappearance in front of him (p.158). But Wes explains to Charlie the importance of using strategic silence to make one's life easier, particularly in their relationship with the volatile Ruth, providing the insight that people often lie or maintain deceptions as a form of diplomacy and self-preservation (p.158).

Guilt and atonement

Key quotes

'And that's my fault, just like everythin that come after. I had a … a duty. To protect her. To help her.' (Jasper, p.189)
'Sorry. An admission of guilt, carved into that tree. Cut into its body, like a tattoo. A word with so much weight.' (p.200)
'I'd never have been burdened with all this stupid guilt. *Sorry sorry sorry*.' (pp.342–3)

Guilt, and its all-consuming nature, is revealed through several characters. Jasper, Eliza and Charlie all feel guilty about their role in Laura's tragedy. Jasper feels that he had a duty to protect Laura because she relied on him (p.189). Eliza's guilt is complex, stemming from her initial ignorance of the abuse Laura was experiencing and her failure to intervene to prevent her sister's suicide. Charlie feels guilt for helping to hide Laura's body, and wonders if he is exacerbating the Wisharts' grief by maintaining his silence (p.162). Jack Lionel is also consumed by guilt, retreating from society because he caused the death of Jasper's mother.

These characters deal with their guilt in varying ways. Initially, the three teenagers dream of escaping Corrigan. Charlie, in particular, constructs elaborate fantasies of life on the road with Jasper or among the literati of New York with Eliza. However, by the end of the novel, only Jasper escapes – and he seems to leave more because of resignation to the fact that he will never avoid suspicion, rather than a sense of guilt. It is implied that Eliza burns down her family home in order to punish her parents for their silence and to expiate her own guilt. Jack Lionel becomes a recluse, consumed by guilt and desperately wishing to make amends to Jasper. Charlie, on the other hand, uses writing as therapy. He finds words cathartic, particularly in Chapter 7: they help him to process the extraordinary and distressing events he has witnessed, and his role in them. Words allow him to 'loosen the valve' (p.329) on his emotions in a way that Eliza seems unable to do.

Silvey also engages with the concept of guilt on a national scale. In his allusions to the historical treatment of First Nations peoples and the significance of the word 'sorry' within Australian political discourse, Silvey prompts discussion of accountability and reconciliation, and the value of apology and of acknowledging collective responsibility. Importantly, saying sorry and seeking forgiveness are necessary steps towards overcoming guilt because 'a good heart won't settle until things are set right and true' (p.263).

Racism and prejudice

Key quotes

'Listen, Charlie we can't tell *anyone* ... *Specially* the police. Because they are gonna say it was me. Straight up. Unnerstand?' (Jasper, p.18)
'Jeffrey failed to make the Countryweek cricket team, which came as no surprise.' (p.164)
'Jasper Jones fell out of the world and nobody noticed. Nobody cared.' (p.394)

Silvey represents Corrigan as predominantly white and racist. Those who are culturally different are subjected to harassment, scapegoating, stereotyping, violence and abuse. Even for those who attempt to assimilate into Australian culture, inclusion is fragile and may be undermined or rescinded, as the Lu family discover. For First Nations characters, the outlook is even bleaker: Jasper's quiet disappearance is a poignant response to the realisation that he will never be free from suspicion and prejudice.

Silvey suggests that racism often stems from ignorance and fear. Part of the reason Charlie accepts those of different cultures is that he is educated and well-read. Reading is 'seeing what it's like for other people' (p.29). In a town where education is treated with derision, many people remain ignorant and make assumptions and misjudgements, such as when the Lu family are assumed to be communist simply because they are Vietnamese. Despite the insight he gains from reading, however, it is not until Charlie literally walks in Jasper's footsteps that he appreciates the ongoing and systemic nature of the racism and prejudice Jasper experiences.

First Nations peoples

Key quotes

'Of course this town will blame him. Of course Corrigan is going to accuse him of this. And it doesn't matter what he says. His word isn't worth shit. All that matters is the fact of this girl's death and this town's imagination.' (p.18)

'And, see, it's these people who expect three meals a day, who got pressed clothes and a missus and a car and a job, it's them that look at me like I'm rubbish. Like I've got a choice.' (Jasper, pp.44–5)

'I matter. And I know I'll be alright. Because I got a good heart, and fuck this town for makin me try to believe otherwise. It's what you come with and what you leave with. And that's all I got.' (Jasper, p.196)

In Western Australia prior to the 1967 Referendum, First Nations people were not permitted to vote. Silvey alludes to this in Jasper's comment that people think he is 'half an animal with half a vote' (p.30) due to his mixed-race parentage. Additionally, he is subjected to racial profiling and stereotyping, and unfairly locked up and beaten by the police, as has happened to many others like him in the Australian justice system.

The only place Jasper experiences any degree of affirmation is on the football field, where his clear skill makes him an object of admiration and earns him momentary acceptance. However, once the game is over, he is 'shunned' by the same people who applauded him (p.79). Symbolising his marginalisation, Jasper seeks refuge in a bush clearing outside of town.

In 1960s Australia miscegenation (mixed-race relationships) was taboo. Jasper and Laura must keep their relationship secret, particularly as she is the shire president's daughter. Similarly, Jasper's father was rejected by the town and by his own father, Jack Lionel (p.313), for marrying an Aboriginal woman, revealing the extent to which those who demonstrate that they are not racist are treated with contempt by those who are.

Migrants

Key quotes

'Jeffrey's parents are Vietnamese, so he's ruthlessly bullied and belted about by the boys at school.' (p.9)

'"He's *involved*. He's red. He's a *red! fucking! rat!*" He leans forward and spits those words at An Lu. "... He probably killed that young girl. Go back to Hanoi, *rats*."' (p.269)

In 1966, just after the events depicted in *Jasper Jones*, the Holt government began dismantling the White Australia policy, which limited immigration opportunities for non-white people. However, this practice did not completely end until 1973, with the official transition to multiculturalism as policy under the Whitlam government. The Vietnamese Lu family is treated with suspicion and subjected to racist prejudice and violence. Like Jasper, Jeffrey endures racist taunts and violent bullying. He is all but excluded from the cricket team, though he is an excellent batsman. His relentless persistence suggests a desire to enculturate into Australian society, perhaps in an attempt to gain acceptance.

With the Vietnam War in the background, the Lu family is suspected of harbouring communist sympathies. Jeffrey is frequently referred to as 'Cong'; An Lu is beaten up for being 'red' (p.269) – a communist; and Mrs Lu is attacked when a local man is drafted (p.168). The unpopularity of the Vietnam War exacerbated racial prejudice against those few Vietnamese migrants in Australia at the time, despite the fact that many who had made the journey were either skilled migrants or refugees escaping war.

Unlike with the First Nations characters, however, Silvey offers some hope for the Lu family. Several characters, including Wesley, intervene when An is beaten and the attackers are denounced (pp.268–70). In the later chapters of the novel, Jeffrey is selected for the cricket team and people offer An replacement plants for those destroyed in the attack.

However, as Charlie notes, such gestures could be considered self-serving, as Jeffrey almost single-handedly wins the cricket match for Corrigan and An's neighbours get pleasure and enjoyment from his garden, whereas no one supports Mrs Lu when she is attacked.

Courage and cowardice

Key quotes

'That's why [Batman] is the most courageous: because he can put those [fears] aside and fight on regardless. My point is this: the more you have to lose, the braver you are for standing up.' (p.70)

'Courage is resistance to fear, mastery of fear, not absence of fear.' (p.92)

Charlie spends much of the novel in a state of fear. Aside from his insect phobia, he recognises that fear prevents him intervening when Jeffrey is ruthlessly bullied (p.9), he shares the town's fear of Mad Jack Lionel (p.21) and, when confronted by Laura's body, he is traumatised by the realisation that children can be victims of terrible violence (p.29). Following this, he is terrified of getting caught for his role in hiding Laura's body.

Throughout his journey of maturation, Charlie comes to learn that many people are afraid. He recognises that Perth was gripped with fear while the murderer Eric Edgar Cooke was at large, and that Jenny Likens failed to protect her sister Sylvia because she was afraid. Even his idol, Jasper Jones, is a 'scared, hurt kid' (p.308) underneath his bravado. Such realisations leave him feeling 'betrayed' (p.308) as the certainty of his childhood view of the world is undermined. Frequently, Charlie says that he needs to 'get brave' as a metonym for growing up (e.g. p.39). Of course, one of his key lessons is that bravery takes many forms, and that courage is something other than mere absence of fear.

Growing up

Key quotes

'My exit from the window is a little like a foal being born.' (p.2)
'Everything in my world that was steady and sure and sturdy has been shaken out of place, and it's now drifting and swirling back down in a confetti of debris.' (p.30)
'I can't unfurl from my cocoon when I'm good and ready. I've been pulled out early and left in the cold.' (p.30)

The challenges of growing up are a central concern of this novel. Charlie begins as a naive thirteen-year-old, who realises his view of the world is limited. As he puts it, the bubble of his world has burst and he can never go back (p.17). Although he knows about bullying and that both Jasper and Jeffrey are victims of racism, the experiences Charlie goes through force him to re-evaluate what he knows about the world and gain a deeper appreciation for the circumstances of others. His confrontation with Laura's corpse is the incident that prompts his initial loss of innocence, captured through the circular nature of Chapter 1 in which Charlie emerges from the window as a foal being born, before returning to it, hours later, filthy and forever altered (p.52). Charlie is thrust into this world of adult knowledge unprepared (pp.29–30) and, like Jasper, has to 'get brave in a hurry' (p.29).

Key point

Over the course of the novel Charlie comes to understand the flawed nature of the adult world, develop his personal moral code and find his place within a society that he recognises is unjust and cruel – all important life lessons in the transition from childhood to adulthood.

Developing a moral code

Key quotes

'… I never stole a thing I dint need … Nuthin big, ever. Nuthin people couldn't go without.' (Jasper, p.44)

'When Laura is just a bundle of lonely bones tied to a stone, do we leave the Wisharts to cling to their threadbare hope?' (Charlie, p.162)

'There's nuthin up there that gives a shit if I took a pack of smokes or lifted a tin of beef. I'm left with meself, and I know what's right and what isn't.' (Jasper, p.196)

Charlie struggles with several moral dilemmas throughout the novel, including hiding Laura's body versus going to the authorities; negotiating his competing loyalties to Jasper, Jeffrey and Eliza; lying to parents and police; questioning the extent of his empathy for distant victims of war; and evaluating the impact of his silence on the Wisharts' grief. Through his research, Charlie learns that some murderers experienced horrific abuse themselves as children, and wonders whether this mitigates their guilt (p.107). It is through his friendship with Jasper, however, that Charlie really comes to develop a more complex understanding of right and wrong. Jasper, for example, does not deny that he is a thief, but reveals the extent of parental neglect that forces him to fend for himself in any way he can. 'Your dad doesn't even buy food?' Charlie asks (p.45), struggling to comprehend that a father could neglect the basic moral duty to care for his child. The small crimes Jasper commits, driven by necessity, are nothing compared to the crimes committed against him by the townsfolk of Corrigan, who wilfully ignore his plight even though they know he is 'an orphan, or as good as' (p.6).

Key point

In their discussion of religion (pp.195–6), Jasper explains to Charlie that morality is a personal choice, that strength of character is doing what one believes is right given the circumstances. This is an example of moral relativism – the idea that there is no absolute system of right and wrong, but that it is dependent on context.

This shift in understanding regarding morality allows Charlie to come to terms with his role in perpetuating the mystery of Laura's disappearance, and enables him to lie so determinedly to the police, to protect Jasper. As Jasper is both powerless and voiceless in racist Corrigan, these acts – that would objectively be considered immoral – are justified in this context.

Charlie wrestles with the choice between maintaining his silence regarding Laura's whereabouts and coming forward, carefully weighing up the pros and cons of disclosing such knowledge and who might be hurt by each option (p.352). As he works through each of these complex situations, he moves from a simplistic concept of morality and ethics, in which sneaking out of the house is his 'worst-ever transgression' (p.10) and reporting crime to the police is 'what we do' (p.17), to a far more sophisticated and contextual understanding.

The power of literature

Key quotes

'[My father] said that Twain was as wise a counsel as any, and that if every man read at least one of his books at some time in his life, it would be a far better world for it.' (p.8)

'That's what you do, right? When you're readin. You're seeing what it's like for other people.' (Jasper, p.29)

'And every night I write stories and poems. I polish my jewels.' (p.76)

The power of language and literature is a theme woven throughout the novel. Charlie learns several life lessons from novels, and many of his heroes are writers. This stems largely from the influence of his beloved father, a literature teacher and fellow writer. The various intertextual references to works of literature such as *Pudd'nhead Wilson* and Truman Capote's *Breakfast at Tiffany's*, as well as the novel's parallels with *To Kill a Mockingbird*, are another way in which Silvey communicates the value of literature: it can encourage empathy and teach us important lessons about the world, such as Twain's maxim that 'courage is resistance to fear, mastery of fear, not absence of fear' (p.92). It is Charlie's understanding of others' experiences, gained from reading, that makes Jasper seek the younger boy's help (p.29). Charlie frequently cites the 'even-handed and logical' (p.259) character of Atticus, the lawyer and father in *To Kill a Mockingbird*, as a role model to guide his own decision-making, trying to 'reason it through as Atticus Finch might' (p.188).

However, Silvey advocates not only experiencing literature as a reader, but also through the power of writing. Writing provides Charlie with a way to process and articulate the trauma in his life. Being bullied for his sophisticated vocabulary only makes him more determined to increase it, each new word 'like getting a punch back' (p.76). He writes 'to make sense' (p.262) of the confusing world to which his eyes have been opened. Wesley, too, writes, and his novel *Patterson's Curse* is 'so smart and sad and beautiful' (p.373) that Charlie feels certain it will be successful.

Finally, the metafictional suggestion that *Jasper Jones* is Charlie's own novel (p.143) also reveals the power of literature. For Charlie, to write a novel would be a test of his own fortitude and skill, a way of proving himself to his father (p.143). For Jasper himself, though, Charlie's potential novel is a way in which his experience might be given voice; he says, 'maybe you could write my story one day'and rather presciently follows up with 'then we'll make a film out of it' (p.47). Literature is an important medium in which the marginalised might have their experience represented and shared with readers, fostering empathy and understanding. Finally, writing is a medium for 'meetin people, tellin their stories' (p.47), providing Charlie with an avenue of escape from the mediocrity of small-town life – an opportunity to 'move to some big city' (p.47). Setting his novel in a town of philistines, Silvey is clearly on the side of those with an appreciation of literature. Unlike the rest of Corrigan, Jasper recognises its transformative power and encourages Charlie in his dream of becoming a writer.

DIFFERENT INTERPRETATIONS

Different interpretations arise from different responses to a text. Over time, a text will evoke a wide range of responses from its readers, who may come from various social or cultural groups and live in very different places and historical periods. Responses by critics and reviewers can be published in newspapers, journals and books, both online and in print. They can also be expressed in discussions among readers in the media, classrooms, book groups and so on.

While there is no single correct reading or interpretation of a text, it is important to understand that an interpretation is more than a personal opinion – it is the justification of a point of view on the text. To present an interpretation of a text based on your point of view, you must use a logical argument and support it with relevant evidence from the text.

The critics' viewpoints

Jasper Jones has been largely lauded since its publication. Michael Williams, writing for *The Monthly*, hailed the novel as 'an Australian *To Kill a Mockingbird*' (Williams 2009), noting that Silvey understands the power of stories. Most positive reviews have praised its social commentary – the way in which it explores the racism and parochialism of 1960s Australia. Others have found its characterisation effective, noting the amusing banter between Charlie and Jeffrey and the more thoughtful, poignant discussions between Charlie and Jasper. Rebecca Starford of *The Sydney Morning Herald* suggests it is 'an engaging historical portrait of an ambitious, intelligent boy labouring often amusingly under the parochialism of an isolated town' (Starford 2010). It ranked eleventh in a 2019 poll of 'Favourite Australian novels of the twenty-first century' conducted by the *Australian Book Review*.

Critical reception has not been unequivocally positive, however. Williams notes that the writing is at times 'forced', and 'the plotting and characterisation occasionally cliched' (Williams 2009). Starford also suggests the novel is 'not without its flaws', labelling some moments puerile and drawing attention to the inconsistency and occasional inauthenticity of Charlie's voice (Starford 2010). Similar criticism is directed at the construction of Charlie's voice by Delia Falconer in *The Australian*, who labels it 'overheated prose' (Falconer 2009). Silvey's success at negotiating the distinction between young adult and adult literature has also been a topic of discussion. Some, like Williams, believe that Silvey 'understands the difficulty of balancing adult storytelling and adolescent protagonists' (Williams 2009), while others, including Starford (2010), suggest a failure to achieve this balance is responsible for the awkwardness of voice that they note characterises the novel. In awarding *Jasper Jones* the Western Australian Premier's Book Award – Fiction in 2009, the judges noted that this dual audience was a strength of the novel, 'defying the notion of intended readership' and praising Silvey's ability to craft a novel that speaks 'to a wide audience'.

Two interpretations

Interpretation 1: *Jasper Jones* gives voice to the experiences of marginalised people, such as First Nations Australians.

Jasper Jones plays an important role in young adult literature, giving voice to the experiences of First Nations peoples in Australia and educating readers about the systemic nature of racism and discrimination that has characterised Australian history. Respected NSW Wiradjuri Nation writer and academic Anita Heiss acknowledges the role non-Indigenous writers such as Craig Silvey can play in supporting First Nations peoples through constructing 'believable, meaningful and (hopefully) empowering Indigenous characters' (Sheldon-Collins 2014). By constructing Jasper Jones as a rounded character, one which directly counters stereotypes of First Nations people, and by interrogating unpleasant realities of

Australia's historical treatment of them, Silvey actively promotes reconciliation, encouraging younger generations of Australian readers to develop a greater understanding of and empathy for the experiences of others.

In foregrounding the role of literature as a method of giving voice to the oppressed, Silvey positions his novel as an exploration of the prejudice and discrimination experienced by First Nations peoples throughout modern Australia's history since colonisation. Jasper recognises that it is through reading that Charlie learns 'what it's like for other people' (p.29) and suggests that the boy could 'write my story one day' (p.47). Avoiding accusations of appropriating Jasper's voice, throughout the novel Charlie allows Jasper to speak directly to the audience through extensive dialogue. In doing so, the reader gains an insight into the prejudice and discrimination Jasper experiences, which includes casual racism at the hands of the townsfolk and violent mistreatment from the police and shire president – the very institutions tasked with upholding justice. Jasper is given the opportunity to directly challenge some of the stereotypes to which he and other First Nations people are subjected, revealing his intelligence and sensitivity, as well as explaining why he is forced into theft due to the neglect he experiences.

In using Jasper as a metonym for First Nations people generally, Silvey provides an insight into the lived experience of those subjected to systemic marginalisation, particularly prior to the historic 1967 Referendum recognising their participation in civic life. Jasper is racially profiled, blamed 'for all manner of trouble' (p.7) and deemed responsible for leading white children astray (p.7). He was blamed for burning down the post office and is aware that he will be similarly accused of Laura's death (p.45). Despite Charlie's journey of understanding, wider society continues to scapegoat Jasper and, in the closing pages of the novel, rumours begin that he is responsible for burning down the Wisharts' house. In a sad indictment of the inevitability of racism in 1960s Australia, Charlie notes that the accusations begin 'like I knew they would' while 'no one casts even a cursory glance' at Eliza, the implied real arsonist (p.393).

Furthermore, in his extensive reflection on the nature of the word 'sorry', Silvey engages directly with the politics of reconciliation. 'Sorry' has taken on a particular resonance in Australian politics, since former prime minister Kevin Rudd's historic National Apology to the Stolen Generations in 2008. Published in 2009, *Jasper Jones* acknowledges the power of apology to 'feel the pulse of other people's pain' (p.263), as well as 'to take blame and admit fault' (p.263), in this case for the historical wrongdoings committed against First Nations peoples, such as the forced removal of children. While this is not what happened to Jasper, the death of his mother breaks his connection to culture and family; when asked about Aboriginal belief systems, he explains to Charlie, 'I never learned about that stuff' (p.197). Saying sorry 'pushes things forward' (p.263), a key aim of the Reconciliation movement. By engaging directly with this dialogue, Silvey participates in the 'small, consistent steps' (Mundine 2020) needed to bring about equality between Indigenous and non-Indigenous Australians.

In titling his novel *Jasper Jones*, despite it being the story of Charlie Bucktin's coming of age, Craig Silvey foregrounds the experiences of First Nations people. In allowing Jasper to speak for himself, readers are exposed to the harsh realities of life as an Aboriginal person in the 1960s. As Charlie comes to terms with issues such as racism and prejudice, so too does the reader, who is led to appreciate the courage and resilience of Jasper as he refuses to accept anything other than his truth: that he has 'a good heart' (p.196) despite living in a society that tells him otherwise.

Interpretation 2: *Jasper Jones* privileges white Australians' experience at the expense of First Nations peoples.

Despite overtly addressing injustices faced by First Nations peoples through the exploration of Jasper's treatment at the hands of the townsfolk, the narrative has gaps that leave it ripe for a postcolonialist reading. Postcolonialism frames a subject in the context of colonial rule and postcolonialist readings of texts interrogate their representations of First

Nations peoples, cultures and histories, as well as how the text engages with or perpetuates the ideologies of colonialism. In an Australian context, postcolonialist critiques often examine the cultural and political meanings of landscapes, noting that these are 'implicated in territorial disputes between colonizers and colonized, marked by ongoing struggle, negotiation and re-inscription' (Xu 2016).

White Australia and its relationship with the landscape is thus an area of focus for postcolonialist readings. Early settlers struggled to reconcile their farming practices with an unfamiliar landscape and climate. This resulted in the landscape being depicted as harsh and unforgiving, or downright hostile. The Gothic depiction of the bush in *Jasper Jones* can be read as reflecting this attitude, particularly when contrasting Charlie's and Jasper's relationship to this landscape. While Jasper is totally at home in the bush, leading Charlie sure-footedly 'despite the absence of any landmarks' (p.10), Charlie instead describes the bush as 'unearthly quiet' and a threatening place where branches and shrubs 'snap back at' and scratch him (p.10). The clearing, a space that Jasper represents as his 'home' (p.15), is 'strange', 'sinister' and 'suffocating' (p.14) to Charlie. Its uncanniness, the very quality that renders it Gothic, suggests white Australia's ongoing anxiety about whether they can ever belong to this land in the way that First Nations peoples do.

Charlie's unease when, after venturing into Jasper's clearing, he says, 'I get the sensation we're being watched' (p.327) reflects the settlers' fear that they were out of place in the antipodean landscape. Gerry Turcotte (1998) notes that a haunting First Nations presence is a common trope in Australian Gothic literature, a reflection of settler guilt over the displacement of the original inhabitants. On some level, it seems, Charlie recognises that he is 'trespassing' on First Nations land, which is now 'eerie' and 'emptier' without Jasper in it (p.327).

Of particular concern in *Jasper Jones* is the ambiguous resolution regarding the title character. Jasper's lack of agency is never resolved, and no one is brought to justice for the violence he endures – he simply melts away at the end of the novel. Charlie notes that Jasper 'fell out of the world and nobody noticed. Nobody cared' (p.394). In stark contrast, Laura's disappearance continues to haunt the town, drawing attention to 'the cultural privileging of lost white children' (Kealley 2021) in contrast to members of the Stolen Generations.

The manner in which Charlie and Eliza take over Jasper's clearing in the bush is also problematic in a postcolonialist reading, symbolising a recolonisation and displacement. Initially, when Charlie first ventures into the bush clearing without Jasper, he remarks, 'it feels like I'm trespassing' (p.327), an acknowledgement of Jasper's prior claim. However, as his relationship with Eliza develops, they return to the 'island in the bush' (p.375) more frequently. The metaphor of the island is deeply meaningful here, standing metonymically for the island continent of Australia, with Charlie and Eliza its colonisers. They gradually take over the clearing, even sleeping in 'the treehollow' (p.275) that once housed Jasper, displacing him even as they continue to refer to it as 'Jasper's glade' (p.376). Eventually, 'it no longer feels like [they're] trespassing' (p.375), suggesting their complete colonisation of the landscape, a move that is treated as unproblematic in the novel.

When read through the lens of postcolonialism, *Jasper Jones'* intent to critique small-town racism, as well as its conspicuous reference to the contemporary discourse of reconciliation, is undermined by the way in which it privileges white experience by focalising the context through Charlie's eyes. In some ways, the trauma experienced by Jasper functions as a plot device to serve Charlie's journey of personal growth, and once that is achieved, Jasper vanishes from the narrative, perpetuating the displacement of First Nations peoples. Jasper is denied agency and, while the structural racism he faces is criticised, it remains largely uncontested – particularly when contrasted with the neighbourhood's strong stance against the violent racist attack on An Lu and his garden. Perhaps most horrifyingly, Jasper is evicted from his home, forced to make way for the one person he trusts: Charlie Bucktin.

QUESTIONS & ANSWERS

This section focuses on your own analytical writing on the text, and gives you strategies for producing high-quality responses in your coursework and exam essays.

Essay writing – an overview

An essay on a literary work is a formal and serious piece of writing that presents your point of view on the text, usually in response to a given topic. Your 'point of view' in an essay is your interpretation of the meaning of the text's language, structure, characters, situations and events, supported by detailed analysis of textual evidence.

Analyse – don't summarise

In your essays it is important to avoid simply summarising what happens in a text.

- A **summary** is a description or paraphrase (retelling in different words) of the characters and events. For example: 'Macbeth has a horrifying vision of a dagger dripping with blood before he goes to murder King Duncan.'
- An **analysis** is an explanation of the real meaning or significance that lies 'beneath' the text's words (and images, for a film). For example: 'Macbeth's vision of a bloody dagger shows how deeply uneasy he is about the violent act he is contemplating, and conveys his sense that supernatural forces are impelling him to act.'

A limited amount of summary is sometimes necessary to let your reader know which part of the text you wish to discuss. However, always keep this to a minimum and follow it immediately with your analysis of what this part of the text is really telling us.

Plan your essay

Carefully plan your essay so that you have a clear idea of what you are going to say. The plan ensures that your ideas flow logically, that your argument remains consistent and that you stay on the topic. An essay plan should be a list of **brief dot points** covering no more than half a page.

- Include your central argument or main contention – a concise statement of your overall response to the topic.
- Write three or four dot points for each paragraph, indicating the main idea and evidence/examples from the text. Note that in your essay you will need to *expand* on these points and *analyse* the evidence.

Structure your essay

An essay is a complete, self-contained piece of writing. It has a clear beginning (the introduction), middle (several body paragraphs) and end (the last paragraph or conclusion). It must also have a central argument that runs throughout, linking each paragraph to form a coherent whole. See examples of introductions and conclusions in the 'Analysing a sample topic' and 'Sample answer' sections.

The introduction establishes your overall response to the topic. It includes your main contention and outlines the main evidence you will refer to in the course of the essay. Write your introduction *after* you have done a plan and *before* you write the rest of the essay.

The body paragraphs argue your case – they present evidence from the text and explain how this evidence supports your argument. Each body paragraph needs:

- a strong **topic sentence** (usually the first sentence) that states the main point being made in the paragraph
- **evidence** from the text, including some brief quotations
- **analysis** of the textual evidence, with **explanation** of its significance and how it supports your argument
- **links back to the topic** in one or more statements, usually towards the end of the paragraph.

Connect the body paragraphs so that your discussion flows smoothly. Use some linking words and phrases such as 'similarly' and 'on the other hand', though don't start every paragraph like this. Another strategy is to use a significant word from the last sentence of one paragraph in the first sentence of the next.

Use key terms from the topic – or synonyms for them – throughout, so the relevance of your discussion to the topic is always clear.

The conclusion ties everything together and finishes the essay. It includes strong statements that emphasise your central argument and provide a clear response to the topic.

Avoid simply restating the points made earlier in the essay – this will end on a very flat note and imply that you have run out of ideas and vocabulary. The conclusion should be a logical extension of what you have written, not just a repetition or summary of it. Writing an effective conclusion can be a challenge. Try using these tips:

- Start by linking back to the final sentence of the second-last paragraph, rather than leaping to your main contention straight away – this helps your writing to flow.
- Use synonyms and expressions with equivalent meanings to vary your vocabulary. This allows you to reinforce your line of argument without being repetitive.
- When planning your essay, think of one or two broad statements or observations about the text's wider meaning. These should be related to the topic and your overall argument. Keep them for the conclusion, since they will give you something 'new' to say but still follow logically from your discussion. The introduction will be focused on the topic, but the conclusion can present a wider view of the text.

Essay topics

1. "My point is this: the more you have to lose, the braver you are for standing up."
   How does *Jasper Jones* explore the meaning of courage?
2. '*Jasper Jones* condemns those who fail to stand up to injustice.'
   To what extent do you agree?
3. 'In *Jasper Jones*, children are more noble than adults.' Discuss.
4. "In truth, it isn't nearly as satisfying as I thought it would be."
   To what extent does this statement represent Charlie's coming of age?
5. '*Jasper Jones* reveals the power of an apology.' Discuss.
6. '*Jasper Jones* is a novel about the quest for truth. The tragedy is that Charlie Bucktin finds it.' Discuss.
7. 'In *Jasper Jones*, growing up means learning that life is a series of compromises.' Do you agree?
8. "Sorry means you feel the pulse of other people's pain, as well as your own".
   What does *Jasper Jones* teach readers about empathy?
9. 'In *Jasper Jones*, all the central characters are outcasts in their own way.' Discuss.
10. "That's what you do, right? When you're readin. You're seeing what it's like for other people."
    What does *Jasper Jones* teach readers about the power of literature?

Vocabulary for writing on *Jasper Jones*

Australian Gothic: a literary subgenre within the Gothic tradition, in which an unsettling landscape is the canvas for exploring cultural anxieties stemming from British and European invasion of Australia.

Bildungsroman: a novel in which a naive protagonist undertakes a journey of moral and psychological growth towards an understanding that allows them to participate in the adult world.

Colonial: a term used to refer to the period of Australia's history and culture following European settlement.

First Nations people/s: an appropriate term to refer to the ethnicity of the original Australians. The text uses the term Aboriginal so this is also acceptable in direct quotations or other close references to the text. Other terms that have been acceptable in the recent past (so are used by cited critics) include Aboriginal and Torres Strait Islander peoples, and Indigenous Australians. It is not considered appropriate to use the term Aborigine due its connotations within Australia's colonial history.

Marginal/Marginalised: literally meaning 'pushed to the margins', this term is used to refer to people in a subordinate position in society, who lack power or are overlooked.

Metafiction: A style of narrative that draws attention to the process of writing or constructing fiction. Charlie suggests that he will write a book, perhaps about Jasper, implying that *Jasper Jones* may be the novel he has written.

Metonymy: the use of the name of one thing to stand for a related wider concept, e.g. 'the crown' for royalty or Jasper for First Nations people.

Motif: a repeated symbol or pattern within a narrative, e.g. the shaken snowdome that suggests that Charlie's world has been unsettled by the novel's events.

Naive narrator: a narrative device in which an innocent or ignorant character narrates the events of the story.

Postcolonialism: an academic theory that is concerned with the lasting consequences of colonisation.

Southern Gothic: a literary subgenre within the wider Gothic tradition that explores the cultural anxieties of America's South, typically focused on the legacy of slavery. Charlie is fascinated with several writers of Southern Gothic literature, including Harper Lee, Truman Capote and Mark Twain.

Analysing a sample topic

"My point is this: the more you have to lose, the braver you are for standing up." How does *Jasper Jones* explore the meaning of courage?

Identify key terms in the topic. Be certain you understand them, and refer to them regularly throughout your essay. Here the key terms are 'more you have to lose', 'braver you are for standing up' and 'meaning of courage'. Consider the different ways in which these phrases are reflected in the novel. What do each of the characters stand to lose? Who demonstrates bravery in standing up? What do their experiences suggest about the different ways courage can be understood? This will allow you to offer a thoughtful, well-reasoned interpretation.

You must also consider the initial statement as a whole, looking at the key terms in relation to each other. Do you agree with the premise that those who have 'more to lose' are necessarily braver than others? In forming your own interpretation, remember that you don't have to agree with the statement wholeheartedly. Instead, ask yourself: 'To what extent do I feel this is true?' This will lead you to question the assumptions within the topic: in this case, that the degree of bravery is dependent on the amount of risk involved.

The topic quotation is uttered by Charlie (p.70) during his and Jeffrey's discussion about the ultimate superhero. A good place to start in your own reflection on the meaning of bravery is to follow Charlie's reasoning that Batman's mortality makes him superior to the invincible Superman. However, this discussion is an allegory for the novel's characters and the various situations that test their courage. Not all of these involve great feats that we might expect of a superhero. Many are quiet moments. Some even involve admitting wrongdoing. Charlie, for example, considers himself more like Batman (p.356) – an ordinary person who must act despite their fears. It is this understanding that gives him the courage to resist the adults in Corrigan and maintain his loyalty to Jasper, keeping his involvement with Laura a secret.

You should also reflect on Charlie's position as a naive narrator, particularly at the relatively early point in his development at which he makes this statement (p.70). He is still quite ignorant of the ways of the world and the suffering of others. Consider whether Charlie's concept of courage shifts as he comes to understand the experiences of others, such as Jasper, Jeffrey, Eliza and other marginalised characters.

Sample introduction

> In *Jasper Jones*, central character thirteen-year-old Charlie Bucktin is preoccupied with learning to 'get brave'. Through his friendships with Jasper Jones and Jeffrey Lu, Charlie learns that courage means persisting in the face of one's fears. For Jasper, being Aboriginal means being subjected to violence and racism, something he has in common with Vietnamese Australian Jeffrey. Charlie himself is bullied because he is intelligent and academically successful, qualities mocked by his peers. Despite the prejudice they face, these characters largely refuse to be brought down, and quietly persist in being themselves. Their marginal status within Corrigan brings their quiet acts of courage into sharp relief, as they have more to lose and, as a result of past experience, know precisely the risks they take. *Jasper Jones* shows us that, rather than involving heroic feats, the true meaning of courage is the continued determination to stand up for oneself and others, particularly when that comes with considerable risk.

Body paragraph outline

Paragraph 1: Outline 'the Batman question' and how the superhero debate introduces readers to the concept of courage.

- Charlie and Jeffrey debate the relative merits of Superman and Batman as the ultimate hero; Charlie argues that Batman is more courageous because his mortality means he is exposed to greater risk of harm but he continues to fight for justice anyway (p.70).

- Batman's courage arises from being 'really determined' (p.69), which allows him to overcome his fear and 'fight on regardless' (p.70).
- Furthermore, Batman is an ideal role model because he 'shares the same vulnerabilities as the rest of us' (p.70), making ordinary people realise that with enough 'dedication and desire' (p.69) they too can be heroic.

Paragraph 2: Explore examples of how other characters demonstrate courage and determination.

- Jasper Jones is a victim of systemic prejudice and discrimination due to his Aboriginal heritage. He is stereotyped by the townsfolk as a thug and criminal, as well as feral (p.6).
- Despite this, he persists in believing that he has 'a good heart' (p.196), a quality he demonstrates in his support for Laura and his determination to find her killer.
- Similarly, Jeffrey Lu is 'ruthlessly bullied and belted about' because of his Vietnamese background (p.9), and excluded by the cricket team despite his obvious skill. This bullying is exacerbated because Jeffrey is smaller and younger than Charlie and others in his year.
- Jeffrey, however, maintains his cheerful disposition, persisting even during the cricket match in which he is relentlessly abused, because he is determined to play the game he loves; this leads Charlie to suggest that Jeffrey is 'the bravest out of all of us' (p.92).
- By contrast, the adult characters, arguably, have less to lose in being brave – such as when Wes intervenes to protect An Lu, but is supported by several others (p.267) – or refuse to act at all, such as Mrs Wishart refusing to testify to her husband's abuse (p.374).

Paragraph 3: Describe Charlie's own journey from lacking courage to facing his fears.

- Initially, Charlie repeatedly states that he needs to 'get brave' and is ashamed that he isn't 'brave enough to intervene' when Jeffrey is bullied (p.9); later, Charlie reflects that it's harder for him to be brave because he is small so is 'capable of being beaten' (p.92).

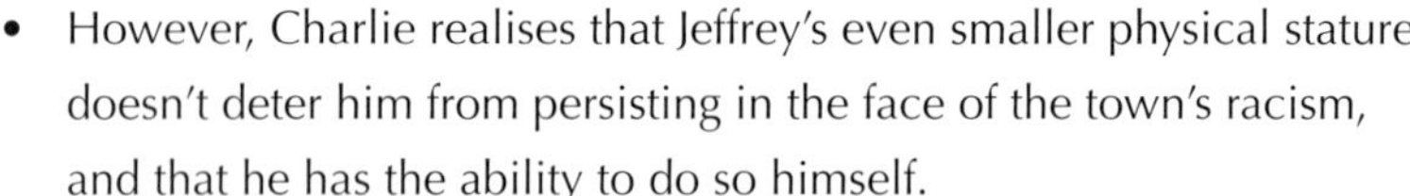

- However, Charlie realises that Jeffrey's even smaller physical stature doesn't deter him from persisting in the face of the town's racism, and that he has the ability to do so himself.
- Readers recognise that Charlie has demonstrated similar determination – even if he doesn't see it himself – both in pursuing his love of words despite being bullied for it (p.76), and in his fierce loyalty to Jasper despite feeling it is 'dangerous' (p.50).
- Realising that Jasper is as scared as he, Charlie reflects on the nature of courage, concluding that bravery is not being without fear, but learning to 'walk with the weight' of it (p.356); he recognises that Sylvia Likens died because sister Jenny 'got brave too late' (p.393).

Sample conclusion

At one point, Jasper tells Charlie that everyone is afraid of 'something and nuthin' (p.30). What marks Jasper, Jeffrey and eventually Charlie as courageous is that they learn to face their fears, which allows them to function rationally rather than be controlled by what frightens them. Their determination and persistence are made more significant in light of the fact that they are among the most disempowered characters in the novel. The risk of further retribution, or the loss of what little social standing they have, does not deter them from continuing to stand up for themselves and each other. In contrast to many of the adult characters, these teenagers seem brave in jeopardising their own safety for the sake of others. Therefore, *Jasper Jones* does seem to suggest that 'the more you have to lose, the braver you are for standing up' by validating those who risk much to stand up against injustice.

SAMPLE ANSWER

"Every character in every story is buffeted between good and bad, between right and wrong." To what extent is this true of the characters in *Jasper Jones*?

In *Jasper Jones,* there are no characters who can be considered completely good. Each character is faced with difficult moral dilemmas where there is no obviously right course of action, and makes choices that in other circumstances might be considered wrong or inappropriate. These decisions are not made lightly, and characters such as Jasper Jones, Eliza Wishart and Charlie Bucktin suffer from guilt as a result of their actions. What they learn is that life often requires moral compromise, that all choices – even choosing to do or say nothing – have consequences, and that even good people can behave in ways that others might see as wrong. Therefore, it is largely true that the characters in *Jasper Jones* are buffeted between good and bad, right and wrong, as they negotiate their way through a complex and confusing world.

While Jasper, Eliza and Charlie are characters with whom readers sympathise, they cannot be considered entirely honest and good. Each makes questionable moral choices and behaves in ways that could objectively be considered 'bad' or 'wrong'. Jasper, for example, admits that he steals, but only what he needs, such as food and clothing, and only because his alcoholic father neglects him, thus subverting the conventional understanding that stealing is wrong. He explains to Charlie that this mitigating factor is overlooked by everyone, who just assumes stealing is in his nature because he is Aboriginal. It is in their various relationships with Laura Wishart, though, that we see how these characters are 'buffeted' between right and wrong courses of action. Jasper had planned to leave Corrigan with Laura, but because he wanted to earn some money and 'be alone for a bit', he went fruit-picking without telling her. This reflects his struggle to do what is right, to support Laura while at the same time wanting freedom and independence.

Unfortunately, feeling she had been abandoned was a contributing factor in Laura's suicide, and realising this leaves Jasper feeling enormous guilt over his actions.

Caught in a similar moral dilemma is Eliza, who followed her sister to the clearing the night she died. Although she could not predict her sister's actions, Eliza too feels guilty for not intervening. But it is her actions afterwards that reflect the ambiguity of the distinction between right and wrong. She spitefully holds onto the letter Laura left for Jasper, knowing this will hurt him, because she blames Jasper for 'luring' her sister away. Similarly, she withholds the location of Laura's body from her mother in an attempt to force her to admit her failure as a parent. Eliza uses her knowledge to avenge her sister and, although she believes it justified, many would consider her decisions morally wrong or even cruel.

Even though we see Charlie Bucktin as a good character who tries hard to do the right thing, he too acts in ways that can be considered bad or wrong. Sometimes this is due to fear, such as when he is 'not brave enough to intervene' when Jeffrey is bullied. However, his acts of assisting Jasper to hide Laura's body and then lying to his parents and the police demonstrate the complexity of morality. Charlie's first instinct when confronted with Laura's body is to 'go to the police'. Jasper, however, knows they will blame him for her death. Charlie is forced to choose between protecting Jasper and maintaining his faith in the authorities. In supporting Jasper, Charlie is hurting others – including himself – as he is 'burdened with all this stupid guilt'. He is forced to keep secrets from those he cares about the most – Jeffrey, his father and Eliza – and worries he is torturing the Wisharts by withholding vital information from them. Furthermore, when Eliza reveals the truth behind Laura's suicide, Charlie agonises over whether it would be kinder to tell Jasper or 'let him believe some other history' in which the reason for Laura's death is not because she felt betrayed by Jasper. The very fact that Charlie wrestles with these choices and, afterwards, is racked with such guilt shows that he is 'buffeted' between right and wrong, and that there is no easily discernible correct course of action.

Wes Bucktin is portrayed as a 'good' character, particularly through the eyes of the son who adores him. Wes is often compared to Atticus Finch, the wise and noble father from Harper Lee's *To Kill a Mockingbird*. Charlie describes him as 'a good and honest person' and clearly sees him as a role model. The two share a love of literature and writing and, in contrast to Charlie's mother Ruth, Wes always treats his son with warmth and respect. Despite this, Charlie finds his father's passive nature a problem, calling him 'bewildered and useless' when Wes refuses to stand up to the overbearing Ruth. Ruth, Charlie feels, has caused his father to compromise his values regarding justice, whether that be failure to protest against the Vietnam War or failure to confront Ruth about her affair. Wes tries to teach Charlie about 'diplomacy' in dealing with Ruth, which Charlie finds frustrating and dishonest. Later, when his parents separate and Charlie reflects on why his father never confronted Ruth about her behaviour, he realises that Wes' motivations are complex. He could have been trying to protect Charlie or might simply have understood his wife's grief and misery. Charlie learns that what constitutes right and wrong is rarely clear-cut. When faced with a complex web of competing considerations, it is difficult and challenging to make a clearly 'good' or 'right' decision.

In contrast, some characters seem to lack any redeeming qualities. The most significant of these is shire president Pete Wishart, a violent alcoholic who physically and sexually abuses his daughter Laura, who consequently becomes pregnant. He put the 'marks on her face' and 'the fear and the poison in her belly' (p.341), unquestionably wrong acts that result in Laura's suicide. But Wishart has no remorse for his actions. After Laura reveals the abuse to her mother, he 'wasn't even sorry' and punches her in the belly to try to cause her to miscarry. Instead of being responsible and nurturing, as parents are expected to be, Wishart is horrifying. Furthermore, he abuses his authority as shire president, conspiring with the police to harass Jasper by locking him in the local gaol and giving him a beating, himself 'sticking the boot in most of all'. Charlie is shocked that someone in a position of authority should turn out to be so morally corrupt, but comes to realise that adult authorities are often flawed. With both the police and the shire president inflicting horrific cruelty and violence on children, it is no wonder that other characters struggle with their own definitions of right and wrong.

In its portrayal of various characters struggling with significant moral dilemmas, *Jasper Jones* represents the ambiguities of our understanding of good and bad, right and wrong. These are not clear-cut distinctions, and sometimes the morally correct thing to do might not be what is usually considered 'right'. Similarly, doing the right thing by one person may inadvertently wrong another. Charlie Bucktin struggles to understand the complexities of morality, particularly in a world where its arbiters are the most corrupt of all and when those he loves are capable of wrongdoing. It is apparent that, in *Jasper Jones*, characters resist simple definitions of good and bad and constantly negotiate a path between right and wrong.

REFERENCES & READING

Text

Silvey, C 2009, *Jasper Jones: A Novel*, Allen & Unwin, Crows Nest.

Film

Jasper Jones 2017, dir. by Rachel Perkins, Porchlight Films and Bunya Productions, starring Levi Miller, Angourie Rice, Aaron L McGrath, Toni Collette and Hugo Weaving.

References

Falconer, D 2009, 'Dudes with attitude', *The Australian*, 6 May.

Kealley, A 2021, 'A Strange Madness: The Lost Child in Contemporary Australian Gothic YA Fiction', in Michelle J Smith and Kristine Moruzi (eds), *Young Adult Gothic Fiction: Monstrous Selves/ Monstrous Others*, University of Wales Press, Cardiff, pp.152–79.

Mundine, K 2020, 'What is Reconciliation?', Reconciliation Australia, https://www.reconciliation.org.au/what-is-reconciliation/

Rudd, K 2008a, 'Apology to Australia's Indigenous Peoples', House of Representatives, Canberra, https://www.aph.gov.au/Visit_Parliament/Art/Exhibitions/Custom_Media/Apology_to_Australias_Indigenous_Peoples

Rudd, K 2008b, 'Apology to the Stolen Generations', National Museum Australia, https://www.nma.gov.au/defining-moments/resources/national-apology

Sheldon-Collins, D 2014, '"Getting it Right": Anita Heiss on Indigenous Characters', The Wheeler Centre, https://www.wheelercentre.com/notes/221927959a6b

Silvey, C n.d., 'Craig Silvey Discusses Writing Jasper Jones', Allen & Unwin Book Publishers, https://www.allenandunwin.com/writers-on-writing/craig-silvey-discusses-writing-jasper-jones

Starford, R 2010, 'Jasper Jones', *The Sydney Morning Herald*, 17 March, https://www.smh.com.au/entertainment/books/jasper-jones-20100317-qfcf.html

Turcotte, G 1998, 'Australian Gothic', in Marie Mulvey Roberts (ed.), *The Handbook to Gothic Literature*, Macmillan, Basingstoke, pp.10–19.

Williams, M 2009, '"Jasper Jones: A Novel" by Craig Silvey', *The Monthly*, May, https://www.themonthly.com.au/issue/2009/may/1241532000/michael-williams/jasper-jones-novel-craig-silvey#mtr

Xu, D 2016, 'Australian Children's Literature and Postcolonialism: A Review Essay', *Ilha Do Desterro* 69 (2), https://periodicos.ufsc.br/index.php/desterro/article/view/2175-8026.2016v69n2p193

Further reading

Australian Human Rights Commission 2008, *Close the Gap: Indigenous Health Equality Summit – Statement of Intent*, AHRC, https://humanrights.gov.au/our-work/close-gap-indigenous-health-equality-summit-statement-intent?_ga=2.224865242.178035324.1630753195-61172067.1616224654

Bradford, C 2017, 'Prizing National and Transnational: Australian Texts in the Printz Award', in Kidd, K B and Thomas J T (eds), *Prizing Children's Literature*, Routledge, New York, pp.33–45.

Cunneen, C 2020, '"The Torment of Our Powerlessness": Police Violence Against Aboriginal People in Australia', *Harvard International Review* online, 30 September, https://hir.harvard.edu/police-violence-australia-aboriginals/

Human Rights and Equal Opportunity Commission 1997, *Bringing them Home: Report of the National Inquiry into the Separation of Aboriginal and Torres Strait Islander Children from Their Families*, Australian Human Rights Commission, https://humanrights.gov.au/our-work/bringing-them-home-preliminary

Silvey, C 2021, *Craig Silvey*, https://www.craigsilvey.com/writer

Tilley, E 2012, *White Vanishing: Rethinking Australia's Lost-in-the-Bush Myth*, Editions Rodolpi, Amsterdam & New York.